The Changing Face of Rural Space

The Changing Face
of Rural Space

Agriculture and Rural Development
in the Western Balkans

Julian A. Lampietti
David G. Lugg
Philip Van der Celen
Amelia Branczik

THE WORLD BANK
Washington, D.C.

Cover photo: © Nyul | Dreamstime.com

ISBN: 978-0-8213-7931-8
eISBN: 978-0-8213-7935-6
DOI: 10.1596/978-0-8213-7931-8

Library of Congress Cataloging-in-Publication Data

The changing face of rural space : agriculture and rural development in the Western
Balkans / Julian A. Lampietti ... [et al.].
p. cm. — (Directions in development)
Includes bibliographical references and index.
ISBN 978-0-8213-7931-8 (alk. paper) -- ISBN 978-0-8213-7935-6
1. Agriculture and state--Balkan Peninsula. 2. Agriculture--Economic aspects—Balkan
Peninsula. 3. Rural development--Balkan Peninsula. I. Lampietti, Julian A. II. Title:
Agriculture and rural development in the Western Balkans. III. Series: Directions in
development (Washington, D.C.)
HD2038.C48 2009
338.1'8496--dc22

2009008533

Contents

Boxes

Figures

Tables

Tables

Preface

Although at different stages of development, the countries of the Western Balkans—Albania, Bosnia and Herzegovina, the former Yugoslav Republic of Macedonia, Montenegro, and Serbia—face similar challenges in transforming and modernizing their agri-food sectors to become competitive in regional and EU markets. Their rural sectors have lagged behind the rest of the economy in growth and poverty reduction, their agri-food sector is undercapitalized and highly fragmented, and their agro-processing capacities are limited. Agricultural trade deficits are widening, climate change is posing increasing risks to farm incomes, and low-cost imports and changing consumer preferences are further eroding competitiveness. Added to this scenario are the challenges and opportunities of adopting the EU *acquis communautaire*, which relates mostly to agriculture: preparing the agri-food sector, including public institutions, to meet EU standards such as those in food safety, and exploiting comparative advantages in agriculture, particularly in the light of the unfolding food and financial crises.

The new EU member states in Central and Eastern Europe faced similar issues, but there are important differences with the Western Balkans. Although governments in the region are unified in pursuing a modern agri-food sector aligned with the EU, they disagree on the most effective strategy and policy priorities to achieve this goal. Advice and guidance are based mostly on lessons from Central and Eastern Europe and the expectation that the Common Agricultural Policy (CAP) will remain the same—rather than the more appropriate expectation that its basic structure will change in the next decade.

In recent years the World Bank's Environmentally and Socially Sustainable Development Department (ECSSD) has published reports covering almost all the Western Balkan countries, collaborating with the Food and Agriculture Organization (FAO) and the European Commission Directorate General for Agriculture and Rural Development. These reports identify the constraints to agricultural competitiveness, examine public expenditures in agriculture, diagnose key policy challenges, and suggest strategic goals, priorities, and policies for moving forward. This report expands on previous findings to provide an overarching analysis of the challenges facing the region's agricultural policy makers and the strategies for transforming and modernizing the agri-food sector that will result in economic growth and a healthy rural sector.

This report comes at a critical time for the region. Government policy and assistance in agriculture have traditionally been accorded little importance, as the weak public institutions and human resource capacity in agriculture show. While the Western Balkan countries are seeing healthy growth overall, agriculture and rural areas are falling behind, trade deficits are expanding, climate change is putting pressure on agricultural resources, and many young rural workers are being pushed to urban areas. The need to meet EU standards in agriculture while addressing the food and financial crises are powerful external forces for improving agricultural policy. Agriculture and rural development as sources of growth, employment, and food security now need to be taken seriously.

Countries are rightly focused on relieving constraints to improve agricultural competitiveness, but this will not be enough to address widespread rural poverty. Households in remote areas, excluded from value chains, may not benefit from agricultural growth. Governments need to think carefully about policies to address these groups, which will otherwise fall further behind.

Another issue is aligning agricultural policies with the CAP to facilitate later accession to the EU. Such forward thinking is necessary—but will be useful only if based on accurate and well-informed predictions of what the policy will look like at accession. Addressing compliance with EU food safety standards before accession is also necessary, but overregulation and top-heavy institutions poorly suited to the region's governance conditions should be avoided. And climate change will have a significant impact on agriculture, with an understanding of its effects and potential mitigation and adaptation strategies being increasingly important.

This report brings together lessons from previous studies, supplemented by new analysis. It frames the challenges facing the rural and agri-food sector in the Western Balkans to illustrate the directions for policies, now and in the future. Part I looks at the characteristics of the rural and agri-food sector today—its potential and its obstacles. Part II looks at the future of the agri-food sector and rural space. Value chains will change with more competitive imports, with larger retailers influencing value chains, and with farmers and processors needing to respond to these trends by producing goods that meet quality and safety standards consistently and reliably. These changes will drive the modernization of agriculture, leading to an agri-food sector with fewer and more productive farms. Beyond the agri-food sector, effective rural development programs will be needed to ensure that agriculture's modernization is balanced and equitable. Local authorities and rural communities will have to be involved in developing and implementing territorial strategies for leveraging the nonfarm potential of rural areas. Food safety standards will become more important as countries strive to meet private and public standards, and climate change will introduce uncertainty and compel farmers to adapt.

Part III provides a roadmap to help governments create a strong and healthy rural and agri-food sector able to respond to these challenges. It looks first at the strategy that should drive public spending in agriculture and the composition of that spending. It then looks at how governments can best provide public services to agriculture, in extension (advisory) services, agricultural information services, and agricultural education and research.

The report's aim is to enable governments and donors to have a common vision of the goals and directions of their policies and programs. It identifies future threats and challenges to the sector—and provides a framework of outcomes and objectives to inform future government policies and donor assistance to the sector. The report and the studies it draws on were drafted in close consultation with governments in the region in order to reflect the concerns and views of its chief audience. It is thus hoped that the report will inform the design and implementation of policies to transform rural areas and avoid pitfalls along the way.

Acknowledgments

The report is a joint product of the World Bank and the FAO, led by Julian A. Lampietti (World Bank/ECSSD) and David G. Lugg (FAO/TCIE). The lead editing team and contributing authors consisted of Julian A. Lampietti, David G. Lugg, Amelia Branczik (FAO/World Bank Consultant), and Philip Van der Celen (World Bank/ECSSD). Other contributing authors were Liesbeth Dries (FAO Consultant) and Emmanuel Hidier (FAO/ TCIE) on value chains; Karin Fock (FAO Consultant) on public expenditures; Marian Garcia (FAO Consultant) and Mary Kenny (FAO/AGNS) on food safety; Christian Boese (FAO/Consultant) on EU accession requirements and agricultural support services; and Renee Giovarelli (FAO Consultant) on land issues. Also contributing were Nada Zvekic (FAO/TCIE) and Jose Mas Campos (FAO/TCIE), who assisted in collecting data for analysis; Richard Eberlin (FAO/REUT) on rural development; David Palmer (FAO/NRLA) on land issues; Goran Zivkov (FAO Consultant) on value chains; Selvaraju Ramasamy (FAO/NRCB) on climate conditions; and Daniel Gerber (World Bank/ECSSD) on climate change. Invaluable comments during the review process were received from Emilia Battaglini (World Bank/ECSSD), Andrew Dabalen (World Bank/ECSPE), David Sedik (FAO/REUT), and Garry Smith (FAO/TCID). The authors are also grateful for the guidance of Claudio

Gregorio (FAO/TCIE) and the ongoing support, advice, and comments from World Bank staff in Washington, D.C., and country offices in the region: Aleksandar Nacev, Irina Ramniceanu, Bekim Ymeri, Ibrahim Hackaj, Carl-Fredrik von Essen, Olivera Jordanovic, Sanela Ljuca, Mirjana Karahasanovic, Samra Bajramovic, and Vito Intini. And without the financial generosity of Jane Armitage, World Bank Country Director for the Western Balkans, and Charles Riemenschneider, Director of the FAO Investment Center (TCI), this book would have been far less comprehensive. The authors are most grateful for their support. Most importantly, the team is very grateful to the staff and representatives of the governments of the Western Balkan countries whose close collaboration and insights into the process of EU pre-accession inspired the book.

Abbreviations

CAP	Common Agricultural Policy
CARDS	Community Assistance for Reconstruction Development and Stabilization
CEFTA	Central European Free Trade Agreement
CGIAR	Consultative Group on International Agriculture Research
EU	European Union
FADN	Farm Accountancy Data Network
FAO	Food and Agriculture Organization
GDP	Gross Domestic Product
HACCP	Hazard Analysis and Critical Control Point
IACS	Integrated Administration and Control System
IPA	Instrument for Pre-Accession Assistance
IPARD	Instrument for Pre-Accession Assistance for Rural Development
IPCC	Intergovernmental Panel on Climate Change
ISO	International Organization for Standardization
ISTA	International Seed Testing Association
LAG	Local Action Group
LPIS	Land Parcel Identification System

PHARE	Poland and Hungary: Assistance for Restructuring their Economies
PPP	Purchasing Power Parity
SAA	Stabilization and Association Agreement
SAPARD	Special Accession Program for Agriculture and Rural Development
TAIEX	Technical Assistance Information Exchange Unit
USAID	United States Agency for International Development
USDA	United States Department of Agriculture
WHO	World Health Organization
WTO	World Trade Organization

Overview

The natural resource endowments, labor resources, favorable climate, and proximity to the EU market give every reason to suggest that the countries of the Western Balkans—Albania, Bosnia and Herzegovina, the former Yugoslav Republic of Macedonia (fYR Macedonia), Montenegro, and Serbia—have potential as agricultural producers and regional exporters. And in the context of the unfolding food and financial crises, agriculture is becoming more valuable in relation to other economic sectors. Farmers stand to benefit if they receive appropriate market signals and if local value chains are efficient enough to compete in regional markets. But since transition there have been inefficiencies and breakdowns in the value chains and significant obstacles to higher productivity in the agri-food sector. Problems in the agri-food sector and general economic and political upheaval have frequently had negative effects on the rural economy. As a result, with diminishing opportunities and falling incomes, agriculture has tended to become an economic activity of last resort, providing critical income to those without other job opportunities. The many small and subsistence or semisubsistence farms in the region are testament to this pattern.

Now, as economic reforms yield higher returns across the region, economic growth is increasing, particularly in the services sector, and incomes are rising. But this improving trend is much less pronounced in rural areas, where growth rates lag behind and poverty rates are falling much more slowly than in the cities. Nonincome indicators of poverty, such as education and access to infrastructure, are also higher in rural areas. With limited economic opportunities, weak public services, and few jobs, many of the younger and entrepreneurial rural people are migrating to cities or overseas, thus discouraging investment and leading to continued low incomes and poor productivity in the rural areas.

These demographic shifts are a predictable consequence of economic change and transformation. But they also demonstrate the lack of opportunity in rural areas. Although farming is a large employer—58 percent of Albania's labor force in 2005, for example—it is not the most dynamic sector. The majority of farms operate at subsistence or semisubsistence, while commercial farms often find themselves pitted against insurmountable obstacles to expansion—little available credit or land, expensive inputs, degraded infrastructure, and poor access to high-value markets. The commercialization of agriculture is often further hindered by the income support received from remittances by older populations in rural areas. Unless these areas become more dynamic, the region risks seeing potentially profitable farmers lose out to imports and smallholder farmers remain poor. By acting as a social buffer, agriculture is effectively held back from fulfilling its potential as a fully dynamic economic sector.

To address the problems facing agriculture, governments have long been assisting the sector with interventions to address specific obstacles—for example, input subsidies, subsidies for particular subsectors, and a slowly increasing focus on rural development. The emphasis on subsidies differs little from governments elsewhere—notably the EU and the United States. Indeed, recent increases in production subsidies and market support in parts of the Western Balkans suggest that subsidies are being ramped up to improve negotiating positions for joining the EU, to benefit from the Common Agricultural Policy (CAP), and to facilitate the shift to EU-style policies. A frequent perception is that maximizing production now will maximize CAP payments in the future, and that the best way to do so is through higher subsidies, as did recent EU entrants Romania and Bulgaria.

But this focus on production subsidies, while politically expedient and representing a rational response to the somewhat perverse incentives of EU accession, may ultimately damage the sector by letting governments, rather than markets, decide on the best subsectors to focus on. Governments worldwide rarely excel in picking winners and may instead cause growth in sectors that then struggle when facing strong market competition. Increasing production subsidies is also counterproductive in preparing for the CAP, which is gradually turning away from them. By the time the Western Balkan countries join the CAP, direct subsidies and market support will most likely account for a significantly smaller share of its payments.

Most important, production subsidies and market support may hold back the modernization and diversification of the agri-food sector by encouraging all farmers—whether commercially oriented or not—to remain in the sector and produce uncompetitive products. The low productivity of small-scale farmers will be extended at the cost of fostering alternative opportunities for them outside agriculture—and at the cost of a more competitive agri-food sector that uses land more productively. Other challenges will make the external environment even tougher for farmers: high energy prices, increasing trade liberalization, growing emphasis on food safety, and escalating climate change. Unless governments equip the agri-food sector to meet these challenges, its competitiveness will deteriorate further.

High food prices are good if farmers receive clear price signals, free of market distortions and replete with market information. As long as fuel prices are high, food prices will likely remain high, demanding efficient logistics and value chains. The potential comparative advantage of Western Balkan countries in high-value fresh fruits and vegetables will then become even more compelling. The fastest and least distortionary way to generate a medium-term supply response in agriculture and to reduce food imports is investment support along the lines of EU programs. The approach requires information systems such as a market information system and a farm registry, transparent payment systems, and a means to evaluate program outcomes.

To become economically dynamic, the rural sector needs more and better expenditures on public goods and services and a policy environment conducive to productivity-enhancing farm and nonfarm investments in rural areas:

- Better roads and irrigation infrastructure, as well as education and health to improve physical and human capital in rural areas.
- An improved business environment and government institutions that entice private sector investments rather than deter them.
- Agricultural advisory services, education, and research to find innovative solutions to the challenges of today and the future and to disseminate them to farmers.
- Encouragements for farmers and producers to make the investments to deal with the challenges.
- Social protection for the vulnerable.

Put another way, rural development policies and support programs, including matching investment grants, are more effective and less distortionary in supporting the agri-food and rural sector than are production subsidies and market support.

Key to any policy framework is striking the right balance between equity and efficiency, often portrayed as two opposing goals requiring a tradeoff. But this need not be so. Here, efficiency means making the agri-food sector more competitive, rather than maintaining the status quo with a predominance of semisubsistence farmers. Equity means ensuring that subsistence and semisubsistence farmers can find better opportunities for income or social protection. This points to a paradox in the needed shift: to make agriculture more productive and competitive, much of the labor in agriculture needs to move to other sectors. This report advocates a strategic framework that avoids the usual tradeoff between equity and efficiency, by pursuing a policy of helping commercially oriented farmers become more competitive, and helping subsistence and semisubsistence farmers find alternative income opportunities and leave the agri-food sector. Broad-based rural development will thus be a key avenue for agricultural development.

Agriculture Is Changing

Agriculture is important in the Western Balkans and will remain so. The question is in what form. Since transition, agriculture has contributed to the economy and supported incomes in poor rural areas. As pre-transition value chains disintegrated and rural areas fell behind because of infrastructure neglect, a contracting economy, and reduced public expenditures, more rural inhabitants turned to small-scale, semi-subsistence farming for income, and commercial agriculture suffered. Now, as countries move toward EU membership, the agri-food sector must shift from income support to a dynamic source of economic growth.

Critical to understanding the agri-food sector's needs is recognizing how it is evolving. Under socialism, agricultural value chains were dominated by large, vertically integrated *agrokombinats*, which were output- rather than profit-driven. Structures included provision of inputs through production, processing, and retailing. After the breakup of the former Yugoslavia these integrated value chains fell into disarray. Many rural residents previously not directly involved in agriculture became smallholders because they had no other source of income. The result was complex and highly fragmented production systems dominated by small, unorganized producers with unsophisticated production structures and quality control systems. Many small farmers operated outside organized value chains, lacked adequate access to inputs and markets, and had difficulty taking advantage of economies of scale. The processing sector, a potentially critical part of the value chain, was likewise underdeveloped, operating without adequate links to a good retail network and farmers who could supply consistent and reliable products.

This situation is changing. The sector is restructuring, and more coordinated value chains are being developed. High-quality, low-cost agricultural imports are increasing, favored by consumers with rising incomes and changing preferences. Integrated value chains able to respond to market demand are now needed for farmers in the Western Balkans to stay competitive. Without value chains as efficient as those of foreign competitors, costs will be too high and products will be squeezed out of the market. Producers, processors, and retailers will need to coordinate more efficiently to minimize transaction costs. This means improving logistics, organization, and links within the value chain. Meanwhile, aligning with EU standards requires better food safety and quality standards, while more investment and consolidation in the retail sector is pressuring producers to provide more consistent and reliable supplies of safe, high-quality products.

The changes needed to improve value chains are already being made across the region, driven in large part by the retail and processing sectors, but they need to happen more consistently to avoid leaving out commercially oriented producers. The upshot of these developments will be a radically transformed agri-food and rural sector: farms and agro-processors will consolidate, leading to fewer large operations; agricultural productivity will increase; and the number of people making their living in agriculture and living in rural areas will decrease. The critical questions in this shifting dynamic are how producers can successfully adapt to this environment and integrate into modern agri-food value chains, how transformed agri-food and rural sectors will look, and how successfully rural economies will absorb surplus agricultural labor.

Fostering Rural Development

A more competitive agri-food sector needs a rural economy that can absorb surplus agricultural labor into alternative economic opportunities. Agriculture is not enough for rural areas to thrive. Smallholders that lack sufficient resources (land, capital, and labor) to succeed in agriculture need alternative income opportunities to avoid poverty.

Governments can stimulate nonfarm income opportunities by promoting diversified and knowledge-based rural economies. This requires investments in rural infrastructure to develop physical capital; improved education and health services to build human capital; land consolidation; and an enabling local business environment that encourages nonagricultural growth through an attractive tax regime, better access to finance, efficient business registration, adequate legislation and regulation (such as protection of quality labels and geographical indications), and facilitation of business partnerships and professional associations.

Beyond the prerequisites for economic growth—a coherent macroeconomic framework, including an open trade and investment climate, a low tax burden, and flexible labor markets—broad-based rural development has been difficult to achieve across EU member states. Important factors determining success include a territorial development approach that empowers regional and local authorities, rural communities, and the private sector to jointly define and leverage their economic potential. This approach helps to adequately identify local potential and needs and ensures that local actors take full ownership of activities. Actively involving regional and local authorities and rural communities has been key to the effectiveness of EU rural development interventions. Such an approach will require changes in administrative culture and institutions in the Western Balkans, establishment of appropriate legal and regulatory frameworks that enable regional and local authorities to actively participate, and support to strengthen their administrative capacities. Programs like the EU Leader+ program have been successful vehicles for promoting rural development using such a territorial approach and could be introduced in the Western Balkans under the EU Instrument for Pre-Accession Assistance for Rural Development (IPARD) program.

Key lessons for successful rural development from other countries using this model include the need for sufficient scale; the need to decentralize administrative functions in combination with fiscal responsibility to endow local players with financial autonomy; the need for sufficient administrative and managerial capacity to prepare and implement complex territorial development plans; the need for organizations that can represent the interests of producers and other rural interests; the need for measures to prevent elite capture of benefits; and the need for proper monitoring and evaluation mechanisms. The best examples to look at for rural development in the Western Balkans are countries in Europe with similar geographic and climatic conditions.

Keeping Up on Food Safety

Governments need to be more aware of the growing importance of food safety for agri-food competitiveness as well as for public health and for compliance with the EU food safety *acquis communautaire*. To build sound and effective food control systems, the Western Balkan countries need a better regulatory framework, effective enforcement and implementation, and stronger control structures. The prevailing inspection, monitoring, and surveillance systems also need to be aligned with international standards, such as the Codex Alimentarius, to make them easy to inspect and a useful framework for producers to follow. The institutional framework needs to provide for coordination at the national level instead of fragmenting and distributing competencies across different ministries. Clear roles and mandates—for example, separate risk management and risk assessment and nonduplicated inspections—are needed for all involved. Better inspection services and laboratories are another requirement. National strategies for food safety control, developed in collaboration with all stakeholders, would help governments design effective systems.

The key messages for improving food safety are that countries should take a gradual approach that accounts for national needs and capacities and prioritizes activities accordingly; avoid overregulation and an onerous food control infrastructure through a pragmatic approach to compliance for small producers and processors; adopt necessary legislation and enforce it; provide financial and capacity-building support for private investments to bring the private sector up to minimum requirements; adopt a regional approach to effectively allocate food safety control resources (that is, use regional initiatives and collaboration for economies of scale); and build consensus among stakeholders.

Adapting to Climate Change

Climate change is the third key challenge facing the agri-food sector in the future. Predicted 3.5–4.5°C increases in the mean average temperature in the Western Balkans, up to 20 percent decreases in precipitation, and more floods and droughts will have significant impacts on the agri-food sector. These impacts may include lower yields, soil degradation, and more pests and diseases—all bringing potentially significant economic losses. Farmers' and governments' capacity to manage increasing uncertainty will determine how well they can adapt to climate change. A key part of adaptation will be the promotion of new farming practices—

for example, different crop varieties, soil management techniques, and more efficient use of pesticides and fertilizers. It also entails investment in improved water use and management, enhanced veterinary and phytosanitary capacities, better weather services, and tailored agricultural research programs. An important corollary to these risk mitigation efforts is effective risk management through index-based crop and livestock insurance. Starting early and integrating these efforts into agriculture and rural development strategies will be key.

The Future of Rural Space:
How Governments Can Adapt and Prepare

All assistance to the agri-food sector requires the right interventions in both substance and overall government approach. To expedite the modernization of the agri-food sector and foster rural development—while still preparing the sector for the increasingly challenging environment posed by modern value chains, food safety standards and climate change—government policies and expenditures need to provide the appropriate incentives for farmers and rural entrepreneurs. They must also be managed in the framework of alignment with EU policies, which necessitates significant changes in public sector support to agriculture. Larger agriculture budget means higher stakes for agricultural spending, making the lessons from this report all the more important.

Current agricultural support must be modified to promote these causes. Subsidies are currently too high and too often linked to the production of specific products and commodities. Increased emphasis is needed on rural development support and improving public agricultural services such as extension and advisory services, agricultural education and research, and agricultural information. Management of public expenditures is also a key concern: budgeting, coordination between sectors (for example, agriculture and education), institutions, and monitoring and evaluation. All interventions should be rooted in a correct understanding of the government's role: to facilitate the private sector and provide an appropriate framework of incentives.

Perhaps the most important point is the need to align budgets not with the current CAP, but with the CAP of the future—when the Western Balkan countries will most likely join the EU. This means decoupling subsidies from production and adopting the principle of the single farm payment; it means conditioning payments on compliance with environmental, food safety, and animal health and welfare standards (cross-compliance); and it means shifting production subsidies and market support toward rural development. Governments should also use EU-type institutions for their national funds so that these institutions are ready when they accede to the EU. These institutions and systems—such as the Integrated Administration and Control System (IACS) and the Farm Accountancy Data Network (FADN)—are the basis for better policy planning and more transparency.

Strategic Framework for Public Policy Actions

Policy Area	Long-term Objective	Key Public Policy Actions	
		Short-term	Medium-term
1. Value Chain Integration	Create an enabling environment for a private sector-led development of modern value chains.	Support formation of private partnerships and associations. Gradually develop and enforce higher food safety and quality standards. Support farmer and processor training on good agricultural and hygiene practices for quality enhancement and food safety. Pilot EU IPARD-type competitive grants programs to support the upgrading of the agri-food sector.	Foster institutions for dispute resolution and contract enforcement. Invest in improved logistics infrastructure. Promote the development of rural credit markets. Implement EU IPARD rural development programs.
2. Rural Development	Promote an equitable modernization of the agri-food sector through nonfarm, knowledge-based growth in rural areas.	Establish the legal and institutional framework for a territorial and community-driven approach to rural development. Strengthen the administrative capacity of regional and local authorities to prepare territorial development plans. Pilot LEADER+-type programs. Improve the business environment by reducing effective tax rates, simplifying business registration, and establishing a legal framework for protecting quality labels/geographic indications, and facilitating private partnerships and associations.	Invest in high-quality rural infrastructure (roads, markets, electricity, irrigation) and social services. Invest in education and research systems and tailor them to the needs of diversified and knowledge-based rural economies. Support land consolidation by promoting functioning land and rural property markets. Promote the development of rural credit markets. Implement LEADER+ programs.

Policy Area	Long-term Objective	Key Public Policy Actions	
		Short-term	Medium-term
3. Food Safety	Develop an effective, EU-compliant food safety system to ensure agri-food sector competitiveness and protect public health.	Develop a lean, EU-compatible regulatory and institutional framework for food safety.	Scale up food safety system toward full compliance with EU requirements.
		Shift to risk-based food safety control systems and exploit regional control capacities.	Implement EU IPARD rural development programs.
		Broaden the scope of extension and advisory services to support the introduction of higher food safety standards by the agri-food sector.	
		Pilot EU IPARD-type competitive grants programs to support the upgrading of the agri-food sector.	
4. Climate Change Adaptation	Build government and farmer capacity to cope with the uncertainties associated with climate change.	Broaden the scope of research and extension and advisory services to support the introduction of new practices and technologies by farmers.	Invest in efficient water use and management systems.
		Align national research programs with the structure and priorities of EU Research Framework Programs and participate in collaborative, climate change-related research projects.	Foster the development of index-based crop and livestock insurance markets.
		Build effective animal and plant health control systems and improved meteorological services.	Promote the development of rural credit markets.
		Mainstream climate change adaptation measures in agri-food and rural development strategies as well as national, regional and local economic development plans.	Implement EU IPARD rural development programs.
		Pilot EU IPARD-type competitive grants programs to support the introduction of new technologies by farmers.	

(continues on next page)

Strategic Framework for Public Policy Actions *(continued)*

Policy Area	Long-term Objective	Key Public Policy Actions	
		Short-term	*Medium-term*
5. Public Expenditures	Align agriculture institutions, support programs, and information systems with the future CAP.	Shift agriculture budget allocations to EU IPARD-compatible rural development measures. Pilot EU IPARD-type rural development programs. Execute national agricultural support programs through EU IPARD compatible institutions and information systems.	Implement EU IPARD rural development programs. Complete the alignment of agriculture institutions, support programs, and information systems with the CAP.
6. Public Services	Assist the agri-food sector in improving competitiveness and enable the rural sector to drive diversified and knowledge-based development in rural areas.	Develop market-oriented extension and advisory services by introducing a multifaceted approach to delivering agricultural extension services. Build EU-compatible information systems to inform agriculture policy. Foster increased regional and international collaboration and partnerships among education establishments. Strengthen links between research institutions, education establishments, extension and advisory services, and farmers.	Foster an environment for private extension delivery to emerge. Complete the alignment of agriculture information systems with EU requirements. Invest in the reform of the agriculture education system in line with the EU's Bologna process and tailor agricultural education and the research system to the new needs of small- and medium-sized farmers in the context of modern value chains, high food safety standards, and climate change. Develop regional research centers of excellence and put in place proper structures to encourage private investments in research.

Rural Areas in the Western Balkans Today

Part I provides an overview of the current status of the rural and agri-food sector in the Western Balkans to show the region's potential for agriculture and how the sector measures up to that potential. Agriculture can be part of the solution to limited growth in rural areas, but it must be given the opportunity to live up to this potential by putting endowments and institutions to work.

The rural sector in the Western Balkans bears many similarities to rural space in Southern Europe about 30 years ago: many small farms producing at semisubsistence levels and a high percentage of the labor force working in agriculture—disproportionate to agriculture's contribution to GDP. This points to the need for a shift toward a more commercial agri-food sector.

Paradoxically, moving people out of the agri-food sector is key. As noncommercial farmers find more profitable income-generating opportunities outside the agri-food sector, agricultural resources will be freed for commercial farmers to expand. The government must focus public resources for agriculture where they are most useful and design rural development policies that assist those leaving the agri-food sector.

CHAPTER 1

Progress, Problems, and Possibilities

The rural sector in the Western Balkans, dominated by agriculture, resembles the rural sector in Southern Europe 30 years ago: many small, highly fragmented, low-productivity farms. Few income-generating opportunities outside farming mean that most rural inhabitants depend on agriculture. Lacking effective social safety nets and lagging behind urban households in income, these inhabitants often end up poor in the absence of any remittance flows.

However, agriculture holds potential for the region, thanks to its relatively inexpensive labor and land, favorable climate, and proximity to the EU. But the sector must modernize. In the last decades of the twentieth century, agriculture in Southern Europe shifted from smallholders engaged in semisubsistence production to a consolidated and hence more competitive sector. In parallel, increasing opportunities were developed for rural inhabitants to make a living outside agriculture. Such a modernization is needed in the Western Balkans. More commercial farms need to scale up and become more productive and competitive, while smaller, less-productive semisubsistence households find a more promising future outside the agri-food sector. As these less-productive farmers leave, the sector as a whole will become more competitive. An intrinsic part of this change is more land consolidation and greater labor productivity.

Key Messages

- Agriculture has potential if key weaknesses can be overcome, thanks to relatively inexpensive land and labor, favorable climate, and proximity to the EU.
- Weaknesses include small and fragmented farms, fragmented value chains, poor logistics, inadequate rural infrastructure, insufficient skills, and a discouraging business environment.
- The sector needs to shift from small subsistence or semisubsistence producers on highly fragmented holdings to commercial farms.
- Modernization depends on opportunities for rural areas outside the agri-food sector.
- Strategic alignment with EU standards and policies will increase agricultural trade and enable EU accession.

The Status of the Rural Sector

Despite impressive gains since the early 1990s and incomes now hovering at pretransition levels, progress in rural areas of the Western Balkans has lagged. One of the biggest differences between rural space in the Western Balkans and Southern Europe is that a higher percentage of economically active people are employed in agriculture in the Western Balkans (about 20 percent) than in Southern Europe (about 10 percent; figure 1.1). This

Figure 1.1. Agriculture Absorbs a Significant Segment of the Economically Active Population

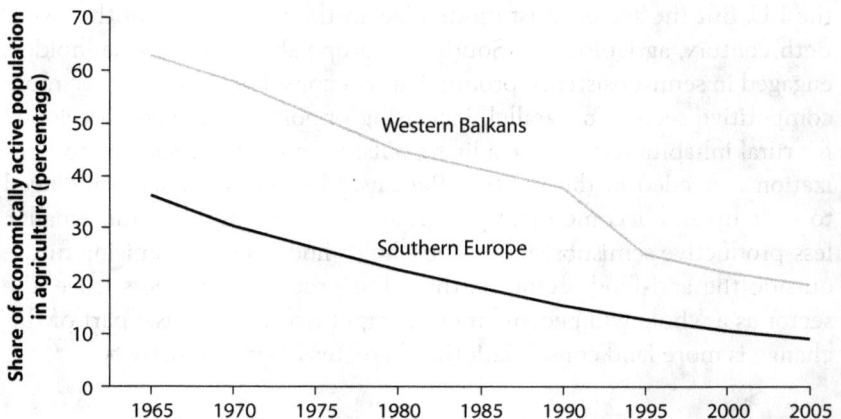

Source: FAOSTAT 2008.

indicates an insufficient shift from agriculture to higher-wage activities and a deficit of alternative employment opportunities.

In addition, a larger share of the population lives in rural areas in the Western Balkans (about 46 percent) than in Southern Europe (about 35 percent; figure 1.2). More striking: agriculture contributes much less to the economy in Southern Europe (less than 4 percent of GDP) than in the Western Balkans (anywhere from 9 to 20 percent of GDP; figure 1.3).

Figure 1.2. A Larger Share of the Population Lives in Rural Areas in the Western Balkans

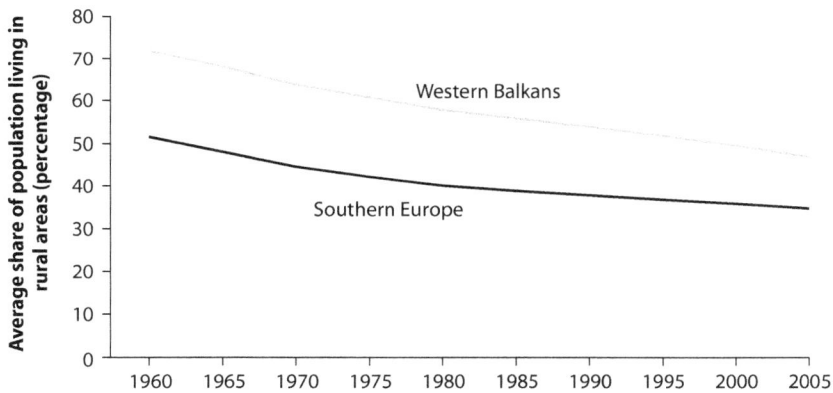

Source: World Bank Development Data Platform Database 2008.

Figure 1.3. Agriculture Remains an Important Sector in the Economy

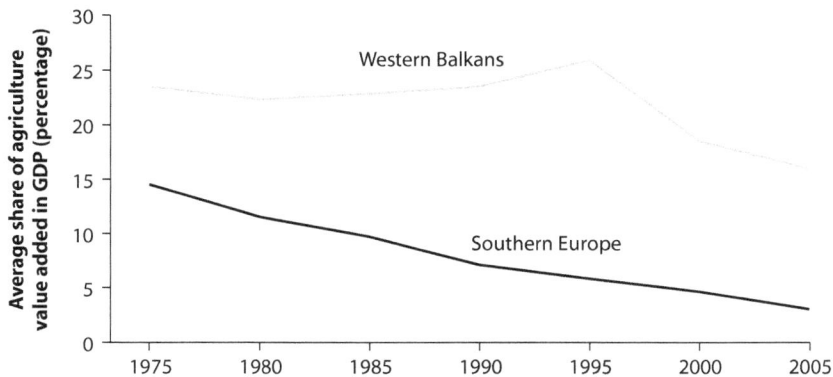

Source: World Bank Development Data Platform Database 2008; USDA World Agriculture Trends and Indicators (1970–91) 1993.

Note: Value added in agriculture measures the output of the agriculture sector less the value of intermediate inputs and does not control for the effect of subsidies.

The rural sector in today's Western Balkans thus resembles rural space in Southern Europe 30 years ago.

Poverty is largely a rural phenomenon in the Western Balkans. Poverty rates in rural areas are higher than in urban areas in all countries (table 1.1), and more than half of poor people live in rural areas. Rural inhabitants are older, have less education, and live in larger households with more dependents than do urban inhabitants. High poverty in rural areas stems from slow growth in the agri-food and non-agri-food sectors and rapid growth in higher-wage sectors in urban areas, including services and construction. Education is also an important determinant of poverty. Skill levels are higher in urban than in rural areas, widening the rural-urban income gap.

Lower living standards in rural areas today are partly a legacy of central planning under socialism. Before transition, farm systems were oriented toward production rather than profit and operated under highly distortive incentives.[1] Agricultural land in Albania was wholly state-owned, while the former Yugoslavia split agricultural land between small private farms and large state-run farms (*agrokombinats*). Transition was expected to boost productivity by allocating resources more efficiently among private farms. But the agri-food sector has had difficulty adapting to increases in trade liberalization and input prices, initial reductions in agricultural subsidies, and the breakup of the vertically integrated state-

Table 1.1. Poverty Is Largely a Rural Phenomenon

Country		Poverty rate at PPP $4.30 per day (percent)		Average household size		Secondary enrollment rate (percent ages 15–17)	
		Urban	Rural	Urban	Rural	Urban	Rural
Albania	2002	53	65	4	5	68	27
	2005	42	62	4	5	78	49
Bosnia and Herzegovina	2001	11	10	3	4	91	85
	2004	7	7	2	2	95	90
Macedonia, fYR	2002	21	29	4	5	91	78
Montenegro	2005	61	65	4	4	95	90
	2006	63	72	4	3	94	88
Serbia	2005	17	28	3	3	94	88
	2006	8	19	3	4	95	89

Source: Authors' estimates based on World Bank ECAPOV Database 2008.

Note: Enrollment rate is based on reported student status. PPP is purchasing power parity.

run farms, which produced the fragmented sector seen today. Moreover, the political and economic upheavals of the 1990s disrupted rural communities and agricultural production systems and had a damaging impact on key rural infrastructure such as roads and irrigation.

Agricultural productivity is low for several reasons. The impressive economic growth since transition has not translated into higher agricultural yields and labor productivity. Take tomatoes, a crop in which the Western Balkans has a comparative advantage, thanks to warm climate and low labor costs. Yields per hectare have grown steadily in Southern Europe but remained virtually stagnant in the Western Balkans (figure 1.4). In 1961 yields in the Western Balkans were 60 percent of those in Southern Europe; by 2006 they were only 30 percent. The trend is similar for various other agricultural products (annex 1, figure A1). This is partly because the agri-food sector has the same characteristics as most other sectors in transition economies: ongoing privatization, particularly of agricultural land (Albania); underdeveloped markets, especially for credit and land; an incomplete and weak legal and institutional environment; limited research and innovation; and a high number of semi-subsistence farmers. All these factors contribute to the underinvestment in production technology and ultimately lower yields compared with Southern Europe.

Agricultural labor productivity is also lower than in Southern Europe, due mostly to the high number of people employed in agriculture (figure 1.5). Agriculture value added per worker in the Western Balkans

Figure 1.4. The Difference in Tomato Yields Is Growing

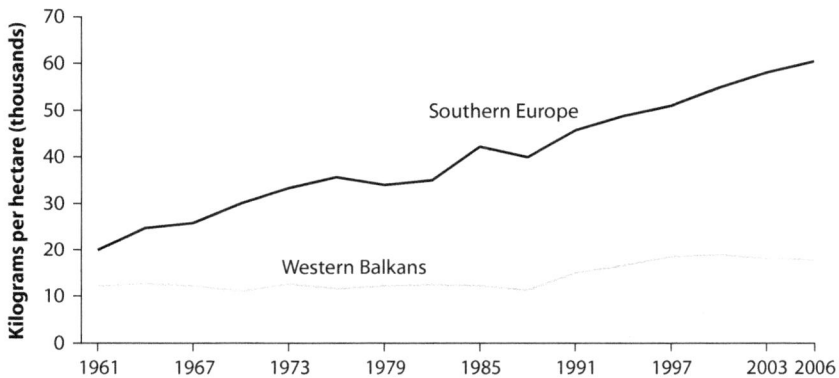

Source: FAOSTAT 2008.

Note: Data do not control for field-grown versus greenhouse technology.

Figure 1.5. Labor Productivity in Agriculture Is Low

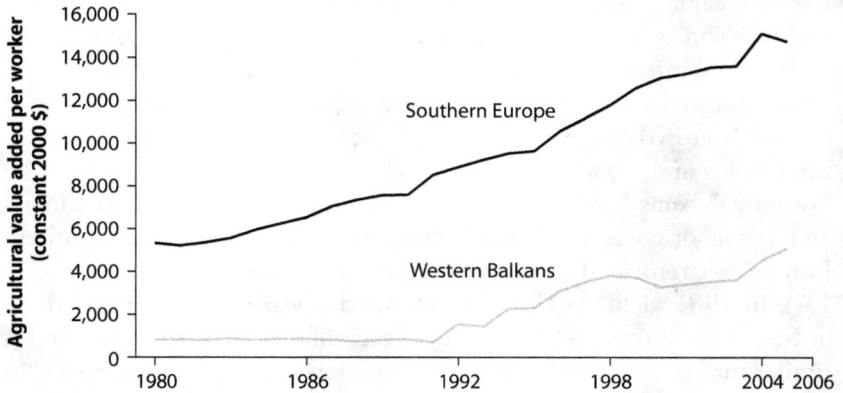

Source: World Bank Development Data Platform Database 2008.

today is similar to that in Southern Europe in 1980 (about $5,000 in constant 2000 dollars). Labor productivity in Southern Europe has risen thanks to declining agricultural labor input over the last three decades, as agricultural workers left the sector for off-farm opportunities. In addition, the rate of change is strikingly higher in Southern Europe than in the Western Balkans, where the rural population depends on agriculture and where agriculture acts as an unemployment buffer in the absence of alternative opportunities. To substantially improve agricultural labor productivity, and hence enable higher agricultural wages, the size of the labor force in agriculture must shrink, and opportunities in alternative sectors must grow.

Farms in the Western Balkans are generally small and fragmented. Average farm size in the Western Balkans today is smaller than in Southern Europe in 1970 (figure 1.6). The contrast between average farm size in the Western Balkans and Western Europe in 2005 is striking: 3.7 hectares compared with 27 hectares.[2] Albania's average farm size is 1.1 hectares, distributed across an average of 3.9 parcels and with an average parcel size of 0.28 hectares.[3] While large farms are not necessarily more efficient, small farms have more difficulty exploiting economies of scale and investing in modern production methods. Some regions and subsectors are exceptions to the fragmented and small-scale production structure. In Serbia, for example, almost 95 percent of agricultural land is farmed by small-scale individual units in the center of the country, but only 63 percent of agricultural land is farmed by small-scale farms in Vojvodina.[4]

Figure 1.6. Farms in the Western Balkans Today Are Smaller than in Southern Europe in 1970

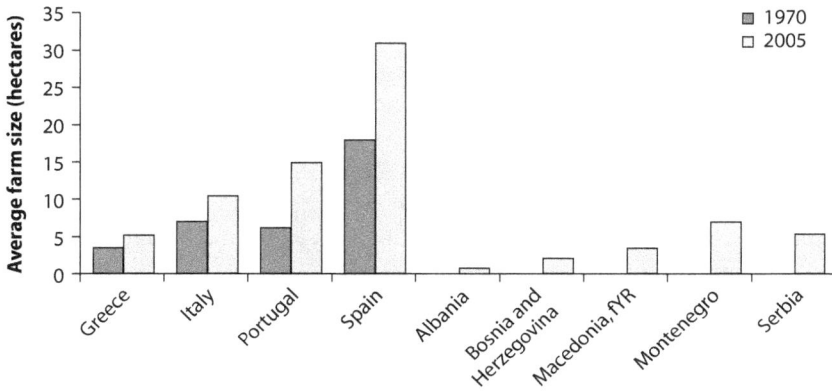

Source: Authors' estimates based on total arable land and permanent crops divided by total number of holdings as estimated by Eurostat, FAOSTAT, and national statistical offices.

The population of the Western Balkans is declining (except in Albania), and rural areas are seeing higher percentages of older people, as young people migrate to urban areas. In Serbia, 7.5 percent of villages have an average age of over 60, and 4 percent have no inhabitants under age 20.[5] The working-age population in the Balkans (including Bulgaria, Croatia, and Romania) is declining, with projections for the workforce to fall from 26 million in 2005 to 24 million in 2025 and to 18 million in 2050.[6] In Montenegro and Serbia the proportion of young farmers (under age 20), as well as those in the most productive age bracket (ages 20–49) is decreasing.[7] In Bosnia and Herzegovina many people who have returned to rural areas are very young or elderly, leaving the most economically active segment of the population underrepresented in farming.[8] This is the group that would normally have the capacity and creditworthiness to develop viable commercial farming enterprises.

Despite These Problems, Agriculture Has Potential

The agri-food sector has potential in the Western Balkans. Almost all countries in the region have seen annual GDP growth above 5 percent over the last decade. Higher incomes mean changing consumer preferences. Consumers are reallocating their food budget toward higher value foods such as fruits, vegetables, and animal products. Moreover, high food prices mean that markets for agricultural products are increasingly valuable. For high-value products for domestic and wealthy Western

European markets, the Western Balkans has potential comparative advantages due to favorable prices for land and labor,[9] good climate, and a strategic location.

Notwithstanding distortions in the land market in both the Western Balkans and Southern Europe, land and labor remain key cost determinants for agricultural products. For the most part they are less expensive in the Western Balkans (table 1.2). Systematic data on the price of agricultural land are limited. However, anecdotal evidence suggests that agricultural land in the Western Balkans is less expensive than land with a similar climate and growing season in Southern Europe but more

Table 1.2. Land and Labor Are Less Expensive in the Western Balkans

Country	Cost of agricultural land, 2005 (euros per hectare)	Gross labor costs, 2005 (euros per month)
Western Balkans		
Albania	7,000	161
Bosnia and Herzegovina	2,500	420
Macedonia, fYR	2,775	343
Serbia and Montenegro[a]	5,000	316
Eastern Europe		
Bulgaria	1,207	161
Croatia	3,600	841
Hungary	1,500	638
Poland	1,700[b]	586
Southern Europe		
Greece	8,765	1,984[c]
Italy	14,266[d]	2,904[e]
Portugal	—	1,557[e]
Spain	16,489	2,135[e]

Source: Agricultural land data: For Albania, Sallaku and Shehu 2005; For Bosnia and Herzegovina: World Bank staff estimates; For fYR Macedonia, FAO 2008; For Serbia and Montenegro, The Financial Times 2008; For Bulgaria, SEE News 2008; For Croatia, Lukas 2005; For Hungary, Popp and Stauder 2003; For Poland, Central European Land Knowledge Center 2005; For Greece, Italy, and Spain, Eurostat 2008. Labor costs: For Western Balkans and Eastern Europe, World Bank 2007b; For Southern Europe, Eurostat 2008.

— is not available.

a. Data are for Vojvodina only.

b. Data are for 2004.

c. Data are for 2003.

d. Data are for 2001.

e. Data are for 2002.

expensive than land with a temperate climate in Hungary and Poland. Differences may be due in part to underdeveloped land markets and fragmentation in the Western Balkans. Data on average gross monthly labor costs for industry and services suggest that labor costs in the Western Balkans are about 15 percent of those in Southern Europe and 50 percent of those in Bulgaria, Croatia, Hungary, and Poland. Agricultural wages tend to be lower than average wages, partly because of the large amount of informal and household labor going into primary production. It must be emphasized, however, that lower labor costs alone are not a sufficient condition for success in the agri-food sector: labor must be of sufficient quality for the sector to be competitive. In addition, despite the perceived low opportunity cost of unskilled agricultural labor, some labor-intensive types of agricultural production experience labor shortages during the peak farming season, as many seasonal workers find (summer) agricultural jobs in EU member states.

Climate conditions in much of the Western Balkans offer natural advantages in bringing agricultural products to the market earlier and longer. The region is warm and has a longer growing season than the rest of Europe. Analysis of daily minimum temperature data over 1993–2007 reveals more frostfree days (daily minimum temperature above 0°C) than in the Eastern Balkans and parts of Southern Europe (table 1.3). Similarly, the first planting date falls early in the southern part of the Western Balkans, similar to that in Portugal and Spain.[10] This is especially important for lucrative early season vegetable and fruit production.[11]

Geographic location in the heart of Europe also suggests advantages in shipping costs to high-value markets such as Amsterdam, London, and Paris. In addition to satisfying growing demand in domestic and regional markets, the Western Balkans may also have export opportunities to wealthy Western European markets. The cost of shipping a container of processed food from the Western Balkans to Paris is about $5,000; more than from Portugal and Spain, but significantly less than from Bucharest, Sofia, and Zagreb.[12]

These endowments might give the Western Balkans a comparative advantage in products that are labor-intensive and that can exploit the long growing season. Such products include early and late season fruit and vegetables. In general, except in the plains of Vojvodina in Serbia, the mountainous landscapes in much of the region do not lend themselves well to cereal production. The region is also suited to take advantage of consumer trends toward organic produce and niche products (due to

Table 1.3. Climate and Location Can Be Important Agricultural Advantages

Climatological station and country	Number of frost-free days[a]	First planting date[a]	Shipping cost to Paris[b] (2008 $)
Tirana, Albania	339	February 9	$5,457
Sarajevo, Bosnia and Herzegovina	269	April 12	—
Skopje, fYR Macedonia	281	April 8	$4,603
Belgrade, Serbia	307	March 28	$5,632
Athens, Greece	363	January 18	$7,403
Lisbon, Portugal	365	All year	$3,372
Madrid, Spain	341	March 3	$3,472
Rome, Italy	352	March 8	—
Sofia, Bulgaria	252	April 10	$8,256
Bucharest, Romania	252	April 16	$8,020
Budapest, Hungary	270	April 12	$8,115
Ljubljana, Slovenia	257	April 14	$7,675
Zagreb, Croatia	276	April 10	$7,982

Source: Ramasamy 2008; shipping costs are World Bank staff estimates.

Note: The first planting date is estimated by an algorithm by Snyder, Paulo de Melo-Abreu, and Matulich (2005), based on the assumption that planting is less risky after the first date with 50 percent or less probability of having a frost event (screen daily minimum temperature of less than 0°C). The listed station in each country was selected based on the availability of complete and continuous data on minimum temperature.

— is not available.

a. Average for 1993–2007.

b. Cost to ship a 40-foot container of class I goods.

availability of labor) or possibly food with a relatively low "carbon foot-print" due to proximity to EU markets (box 1.1).[13]

The Main Obstacles to a Healthy Agricultural Sector

Despite the Western Balkans' agricultural potential, the region is a net food importer (table 1.4), and agricultural exports constitute only a small portion of total exports. Imports are not limited to cereals and include high-value products such as fruits, fruit juices, vegetables, and meat. In 2003 exports of high-value agri-food products were only about a third of imports of these products from the EU.[14] The position has worsened in recent years, particularly in Bosnia and Herzegovina and fYR Macedonia, with exports of some agricultural products falling and imports generally rising. The exception is Serbia, which exports substantial amounts of

Box 1.1

The Western Balkans Are Well Placed to Respond to Increasing Demand for "Environmentally Sustainable" Products

Shifting consumer trends in Western Europe over the past decade strikingly illustrate the opportunities available to Western Balkans producers if the agri-food sector could respond to demand. Organic produce, whose market has expanded significantly, uses few inputs and abundance of labor, suggesting that the Western Balkans could do well in this market. Another trend is demand for environmentally friendly products, such as animals that have not been intensively reared or foods with a low "carbon footprint." This is frequently measured by the distance food has traveled. The Western Balkans could again take advantage of its proximity to high-value EU markets to capture more of this market. Another possibility is to take greater advantage of the marketing potential from designating products under the EU's product of designated origin rules.

Table 1.4. Despite Potential Advantages, Western Balkan Countries Import Most of their Food, 2003–05

Country	Net cereal imports ($ millions)	Agricultural imports ($ millions)	Agricultural exports ($ millions)	Agricultural exports as a share of total exports (percent)
Albania	104	351	41	10
Bosnia and Herzegovina	119	816	114	7
Macedonia, fYR	43	377	216	13
Serbia and Montenegro[a]	−100	767	814	20

Source: World Bank 2007f.

a. Although Montenegro declared independence from Serbia and Montenegro on June 3, 2006, disaggregated data for each country are not available.

cereals, especially from the flat and fertile plains of Vojvodina. Serbia is also a net exporter of vegetables to the EU.

Though the region has the land, labor, location, and climate needed for a vibrant agri-food sector that supplies domestic and European markets with high-value products, obstacles remain. These include underdeveloped rural land markets, inadequate coordination in the value chain, poor logistics and infrastructure, insufficient skills, and a cumbersome business environment—all of which undermine agri-food productivity growth and incentives for producers and processors to innovate.

Poorly defined property rights and weak institutions that encourage informal transactions continue to limit development of rural land markets, which in turn limits land consolidation. Land is less likely to be allocated to the most efficient use, and farmers who are willing to scale up commercial operations may be unable to access land. Formal legislation is in place to support an active land market in most Western Balkan countries, but implementation is problematic. Property rights remain poorly defined for several reasons. While there has been a long tradition of private land ownership, the countries of the former Yugoslavia have struggled with privatizing collective farms.[15] In Albania more than 90 percent of farms claim to own their land, but the share of households with formal land rights varies and diminishes with smaller land size. With privately held land, after owners die their heirs may not take the property because of institutional requirements or inheritance disputes. In the former Yugoslavia land may have been sold or subdivided without registering the transaction or property records may have been destroyed.[16] Land markets also affect credit markets because agricultural producers normally use land as collateral for loans.

Fragmentation across the value chain raises production costs and reduces competitiveness. Transition has affected both primary producers and agro-processors and retailers and splintered the value chain from primary producers to retailers. Prior to the breakup of the former Yugoslavia, investments in the sunflower-seed-crushing industry were made based on a centrally planned system of production in Croatia and crushing in Serbia.[17] The result today is excess production capacity in Croatia and excess crushing capacity in Serbia. Such problems are compounded by overemployment in formerly socially owned enterprises that are being privatized.

The processing sector that has emerged from the transition is extremely fragmented. One Serbian company, the Danube Food Group, processes 47 percent of all milk in Serbia, but the rest is processed by some 219 dairies, 200 of which are unlikely to be commercially viable in the long run.[18] Bosnia and Herzegovina had only 18 large-scale flour and feed mills in 1995; today it has 78, an increase driven mainly by the establishment of small private mills after the war.[19] By contrast, the tobacco and beer industries have recovered and grown. Mineral water production and juice factories, though newly established, have grown substantially. And after initial difficulties, the dairy sector has mostly recovered and accounts for significant investments.

The current business environment is too expensive and time consuming and discourages investment. In an average Western Balkan city it takes 27 days, 10 procedures, and 21 percent of per capita income to start a new business.[20] This performance is 114 out of 178 representative cities worldwide. There is, however, significant variation across the Western Balkans due to differing municipal and national regulations for registration, inspection by authorities, fees, and registration with the health fund, tax authority, and social security.

One result is low foreign investment in the region. Starting from roughly similar levels in the early 1990s, investment in new EU member states has risen considerably while lagging in the Western Balkans.[21] And more than 80 percent of investment that did go to the Balkans region went to Bulgaria, Croatia, and Romania. Improving the business environment thus remains an important priority, including at the local level in the context of rural development programs (see chapter 3).

With modern value chains and global markets, logistics—including efficient customs, good transport and information technology, and timely shipments—are needed to realize potential comparative advantages in the agri-food sector. Logistics mean that goods are delivered predictably, efficiently, and cost-effectively. They also increase competition among traders, processors, and retailers, ultimately enabling primary producers to take a larger share of retail prices. Countries in the Western Balkans face several disadvantages (table 1.5). They are in the bottom half of the world in overall performance of logistics infrastructure, with missed opportunities for supplying both domestic and international markets.[22]

Upgrading infrastructure is critical for both the agri-food and non-agri-food sectors, which need access to high-quality infrastructure to efficiently link to domestic and foreign markets and remain competitive. This includes reliable water, electricity, telephony, and transportation, all of which are insufficient due in part to lack of operations and maintenance. Despite relatively high public investment, many Western Balkan countries still face infrastructure constraints in scope and quality. For example, fixed-line and mobile phone penetration is among the lowest in the region, and mobile and long distance rates are extremely high. Internet access is growing rapidly but remains minimal, and the reliability of telecommunication services is low. Energy supply is a top

Table 1.5. The Western Balkans Are Not Connected to Compete

| Country | 2007 Logistics performance index[a] | |
	Rank (out of 150 countries)	Score
Western Balkans		
Albania	139	2.08
Bosnia and Herzegovina	88	2.46
Macedonia, fYR	90	2.43
Serbia and Montenegro[b]	115	2.28
Eastern Europe		
Bulgaria	55	2.87
Croatia	63	2.71
Hungary	35	3.15
Poland	40	3.04
Southern Europe		
Greece	29	3.36
Italy	22	3.58
Portugal	28	3.38
Spain	26	3.52

Source: World Bank, 2007f.

a. The logistics performance index is built on information from a web-based questionnaire completed by more than 800 logistics professionals worldwide. The index uses seven areas of performance as indicators: efficiency of the clearance process by customs and other border agencies, quality of transport and information technology infrastructure for logistics, ease and affordability of arranging international shipments, competence of the local logistics industry, ability to track and trace international shipments, domestic logistics costs, and timeliness of shipments in reaching destination.

b. Although Montenegro declared independence from Serbia and Montenegro on June 3, 2006, disaggregated data for each country are not available.

constraint for doing business, especially for small and medium-size enterprises. In Kosovo unreliable energy supply has led to annual losses of about 5 percent of sales.[23] Again, public investment could make an enormous difference.

Government and the Rural Sector

Government support to the rural sector has come a long way, from command-and-control policies under socialism to support for transition, often assisted by the donor community. Government policies have included changing the structure of the sector, with privatization altering land ownership and use. Assistance long focused on boosting agricultural productivity, but today it is increasingly framed by the broader economic and political context of EU pre-accession. This section looks at how the intersection between the agri-food sector and government has evolved and how assistance to agriculture fits into the region's EU aspirations.

From Emergency Relief to Promoting Commercial Agriculture

Governments in the Western Balkans have been addressing the problems in the agri-food sector since the beginning of transition. The first phase of interventions (1991–2000) responded to the immediate political and economic crises by providing emergency relief and key production resources for farmers. Governments funded imports of agricultural inputs, provided access to credit, rehabilitated key rural infrastructure, and helped establish the institutional framework for a market-based economy. Structural adjustment programs supported the transition from a central-planning to a market-based production system, including privatization of state-owned farms.

The second phase (2001–06) addressed key constraints to a commercial agri-food sector. Investment and technical support programs promoted efficient markets for land and inputs such as fertilizer and seed, irrigation and rural infrastructure, agricultural services, integrated value chains, and improved farm technologies, management, and marketing skills. These programs aimed to boost productivity and competitiveness through market-oriented institutional reforms and capacity-building, as well as investment support and technical assistance to farmers, processors, and farmer organizations.

Moving toward the EU

The Western Balkans region is now looking toward the EU to transform the agri-food sector. Public programs to alleviate emergency needs and help resume positive agricultural growth after the political and economic crises of the 1990s are finished. Having signed Stabilization and Association Agreements (SAAs) paving the way for EU accession, governments are formulating new strategies for the public sector in agriculture and rural development, and are adopting principles for public spending that are largely consistent with the CAP and harmonization with the *acquis communautaire* (see table A.1 and A.2 in annex 1). The CAP increasingly emphasizes spending on rural development (so-called Pillar 2 spending), suggesting that support in the Western Balkans will shift increasingly from direct subsidies and market support to rural development, though specific measures, delivery methods, institutional settings, and coordination mechanisms have yet to be fully defined.

After aligning with EU pre-accession requirements to help realize their goal of joining the EU, countries will need to make the best use of available EU financing to consolidate and modernize their agri-food and rural sector in order to thrive in a demanding and competitive market. Critical actions include reducing farm fragmentation to improve primary production, boosting labor productivity by creating opportunities outside agriculture, maximizing comparative advantages by investing in food quality and safety, and adapting to climate change.

Annex 1. Supplemental Figures and Tables

Figure A1. Yield Differences Are Growing for Various Agricultural Products

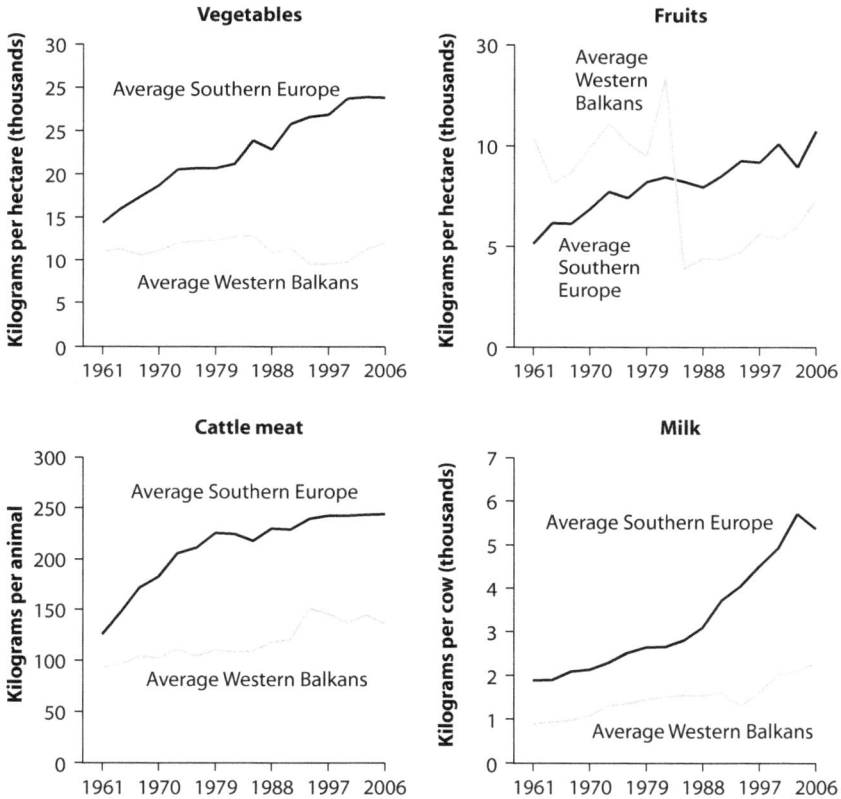

Source: FAOSTAT 2008.

Note: The precipitous fall in fruit yields is likely due to a combination of factors associated with the collapse of the former Yugoslavia, including changes in recordkeeping and the breakup of collective farms.

Table A1. Agriculture and Rural Development Strategies in the Western Balkans

Country	Agriculture strategy documents	Rural development strategy documents
Albania	Ministry of Agriculture, Food and Consumer Protection *Sector Strategy of Agriculture and Food (SSAF)* May 2007 Draft	Ministry of Agriculture, Food and Consumer Protection *Inter-sectoral Rural Development Strategy of Albania, ISRDSA 2007–2013* March 2007 Draft
Bosnia and Herzegovina	State Level Ministry of Foreign Trade and Economic Relations, Sector for Agriculture, Food, Forestry, and Rural Development *Agricultural Sector Development Strategy* December 2004 Draft Federation of Bosnia and Herzegovina (FBiH) Ministry of Agriculture, Water Management and Forestry of the Federation of Bosnia and Herzegovina *Mid Term Strategy for Development of the Agriculture Sector in FBiH (2006–2010)* Adopted in 2006 Republika Srpska Ministry of Agriculture, Forestry and Water Management of the Republika Srpska *Strategy for Agricultural Development of the Republic of Srpska by 2015* Adopted in 2006 District of Brcko Department of Agriculture, Forestry and Water Management, District of Brcko *Development Strategy for Agriculture* Drafted but not yet adopted (expected for February/March 2008)	State Level Ministry of Foreign Trade and Economic Relations, Sector for Agriculture, Food, Forestry, and Rural Development *BiH Strategic Plan for Harmonization of Agriculture, Food, and Rural Development (2008–2010)* September 2007 Draft, working document
Macedonia, fYR	Ministry of Agriculture, Forestry, and Water Economy *National Agricultural and Rural Development Strategy (NARDS) For The Period 2007–2013* Draft February 2007	Combined with agricultural strategy

Country	Agriculture strategy documents	Rural development strategy documents
Montenegro	Ministry of Agriculture, Forestry and Water Management *Montenegro's Agriculture and Rural Development Strategy 2007–2013* Adopted in 2006	Combined with agricultural strategy
Serbia	Ministry of Agriculture, Forestry and Water Management *Agricultural Strategy Republic of Serbia* Adopted in 2005.	National Rural Development Program for 2008-2013 (March 2008 Draft, adoption pending)

Source: Agriculture and rural development strategies of Albania, Bosnia and Herzegovina, fYR Macedonia, Montenegro, and Serbia.

Table A2. West Balkan Agriculture and Rural Development Strategy Objectives and EU Common Agriculture Policy

Country	Pillar 1 Agricultural and market support		Pillar 2 Rural development		
	Direct payments	Market support	Axis 1 competitiveness	Axis 2 environment (Axis 4 LEADER)	Axis 3 diversification
Albania	Strategic goal.	Identifies strategic sectors for support.	Strategic goal 3. Strategic goal 5.	Strategic goal 1.	Platform for rural innovation.
Bosnia and Herzegovina	4th priority axis.	3rd priority axis.	Strategic goal a.	Strategic goal e (p. 153). 5th priority axis (p. 154).	Strategic goal c (p. 153). 6th priority axis (p. 154).
Macedonia, fYR	"Improve farm incomes" is part of policy objective statement. Support policy will shift to decoupled payments.	Anticipates support to a number of specific products (pp. 70–71).	Part of policy objective statement (p. 62).	Part of policy objective statement (p. 62).	Part of policy objective statement (p. 62).
Montenegro	To be gradually strengthened as instruments (p. 101). Envisaged to be the only instrument used in the future (p. 110).	Not anticipated.	Objective 4 (p. 98). Part of rural development policy to be strengthened (p.101).	Objective 1 (p. 98). Part of rural development policy to be strengthened (p.101).	Objective 3 (p. 98). Part of rural development policy to be strengthened (p.101).
Serbia	3rd strategic goal (p. 13).	3rd strategic goal (p. 13).	1st strategic goal (p. 13).	5th strategic goal (p. 13).	4th strategic goal (p. 3).

Source: Agriculture and rural development strategies of Albania, Bosnia and Herzegovina, fYR Macedonia, Montenegro, and Serbia.

Notes

1. World Bank 2008f.

2. Average farm size is calculated as the total area of arable land and permanent crops divided by the total number of holdings; it does not reflect land fragmentation.

3. World Bank 2007e.

4. World Bank 2003b.

5. Marosan and others 2007.

6. Muenz 2007.

7. European Commission 2006b.

8. The most economically active sector of the population in Bosnia and Herzegovina is ages 25–49 (European Commission 2006c).

9. Overall employment levels for the Western Balkans are low, and unemployment levels are high, suggesting labor supply is not a constraint.

10. Snyder and others 2005.

11. These data are for capital cities, which are not always located in the prime agricultural areas, and generally underestimate the first planting date and the length of growing season. The first planting date is estimated solely by daily minimum temperature and in the regions with strong influence of the Mediterranean Sea; the growing season is more often limited by low summer precipitation than by temperature.

12. Very small amounts of produce enter Europe from North Africa.

13. Garside and others 2008.

14. Eurostat 2005. Includes live animals, animal products, vegetables, and foodstuffs including beverages, spirits, and tobacco.

15. Rabinowicz and others 2006; World Bank 2006a, 2006b.

16. In Albania customary, informal, and nontransparent relationships dominate and will cease only when the state land administration functions transparently and efficiently. The supply of land for sale is also low, possibly because land provides a social safety net for many, which suggests efforts should focus on improving the rental market. Bosnia and Herzegovina's formal land sales and rental sector is inefficient, charges high fees and taxes, and lacks transparency, encouraging informal transactions and illegal developments. In fYR Macedonia, many land transactions are not registered, and cadastre and other records are incomplete and out-of-date, leading to uncertainty and a lack of trust in the property markets. In Serbia, transactions are usually based on unregistered contracts and paid in-kind rather than with cash. Farmers demonstrate little understanding of land market price formation (World Bank 2006b).

17. FAO 2001.

18. Government of Serbia 2008a.

19. CEEC AGRI POLICY 2006a.

20. World Bank 2008c. This figure includes Croatia.

21. Baourakis and others 2006; World Bank 2006c. There is considerable hetero-geneity in recent values, with Montenegro and Serbia receiving much more investment than Albania, Bosnia and Herzegovina, and fYR Macedonia.

22. This is another critical area, also addressed in chapter 3, where subnational initiatives could improve competitiveness.

23. This does not include the cost of purchasing and operating backup genera-tors. World Bank 2003a.

PART II

Rural Areas in the Future

After part I's review of the characteristics of today's rural and agri-food sectors, part II turns to how the agri-food sector will look in the future and what challenges it will face.

Chapter 2 examines the development of and challenges associated with value chains. Transforming value chains will be the most formative factor in shaping agriculture. As consumer incomes grow and demand increases, retailers will respond by sourcing products from consistent, high-quality, and reliable suppliers. Facing stiffer competition from low-cost and high-quality imports, local producers will have to improve their competitiveness to maintain market share. One way to do so is to improve value-chain coordination with better links between farmers, processors, and retailers (vertical integration) and among farmers (horizontal integration). Consolidation in the sector will also lead to fewer, more productive, farms and processors.

To ensure that modernization is balanced and equitable, smallholder farmers who leave the agri-food sector must have sufficiently rewarding nonfarm alternatives. Diversified and knowledge-based rural economies, closely integrated with regional urban networks, could help achieve this. Chapter 3 looks at the policy challenges and investment priorities associated with promoting a dynamic rural space in the Western Balkans that goes beyond the agri-food sector.

Another major challenge will be increasing the focus on food safety standards in response to consumer preferences, public health threats, and EU standards. Chapter 4 looks at the policy challenges associated with these food safety needs.

The final major challenge for the agri-food sector will be climate change, leading to warmer temperatures, less precipitation, and greater frequency of droughts and floods in the Western Balkans. Chapter 5 focuses on the sector's need to manage and mitigate the impact of climate change.

CHAPTER 2

The Future of Agriculture

Consumer preferences in the Western Balkans are shifting toward higher quality and safer food products. This pressures retail suppliers to respond, which in turn pressures primary producers. Increasing competition from imports will force farmers and agro-processors to adapt or leave the market.

Value chains in the Western Balkans used to be dominated by large, vertically integrated *agrokombinats* that were output- rather than profit-driven. Integrated value chains that respond to market demand are now gradually emerging. To adapt to changing consumer preferences, farmers, processors, and retailers need to consolidate and integrate vertically and horizontally to improve quality standards, reduce costs, and boost competitiveness. This will transform agri-food production and ultimately rural areas.

This chapter looks at the changes in the agri-food sector, the factors driving these changes, and the future of the sector. It reviews lessons learned from the impact of these trends on small farmers in EU member states and how producers adapted.

Key Messages

- Modern agri-food value chains now developing in the Western Balkans are transforming the agri-food and rural sectors and will result in more competitive, consolidated farms and processors.
- The development of value chains is driven primarily by consumer demand. International and local food retailers who can source both domestically and internationally and seek reliable high-quality products (safe, consistent, and delivered on time) are imposing higher food

quality and safety requirements under the general framework of EU rules and regulations designed to protect consumers.

- Modern agri-food value chains are led by downstream segments: food retailers and agro-processors. The development of these chains is dependent on the private sector; governments should not intervene, just create an enabling environment.

How Demand and Competition Are Driving Change

Value chains are forms of industrial organization that, when properly developed, can greatly improve the effectiveness with which farmers are able to access markets, their productivity, and the efficiency of markets themselves.[1] Value-chain development enables farmers to participate in assured, higher-value markets, with positive effects on the prices they receive. Value-chain development can also have a positive effect on rural employment, by increasing on farm high-value production and by bringing processing, where feasible, closer to the farm gate. Farmers can participate in value chains through such means as contract farming or partial or total ownership of value-chain functions such as transportation, storage, processing, and other marketing functions. The final form of a value chain depends on the product, available technology, and entrepreneurship and on whether a new value chain needs to be created or an existing chain can be realigned.

Several factors are redefining agri-food value chains and modernizing the agri-food sector in the Western Balkans. Changing consumer demand is one of the major drivers, a response to higher incomes and a greater preference for safe, high-quality food. This has important consequences for all levels of the food chain: farms, processors, and retailers. As consumers increasingly demand safe food, retailers demand that their suppliers produce under hygienic conditions, support traceability (the ability to trace the history of a food product), and require products to be delivered at the right time and in sufficient quantity and quality (a parameter that includes safety). Trade liberalization means that high-quality, low-price products can be sourced inexpensively from the EU and elsewhere. This pressures local producers to increase quality to compete in the market, driving restructuring of the sector and encouraging value-chain coordination.

Changing Consumer Preferences Are Driving the Market
Affluent consumers in Western Europe are increasingly emphasizing convenience and health and environmental implications of their food

products rather than simply price. As incomes rise, time spent preparing food decreases and one-stop shopping, processing, and in-store food preparation become more important. Wealthier and better educated consumers search for healthier food options, and concern about food quality and safety increases. Some 42 percent of EU consumers believe that they are at risk of a negative health effect from their food.[2] While the CAP used to focus on food security and farmer livelihoods, EU citizens now believe that its primary aim should be to ensure healthy and safe food.[3] Consumer concerns extend to the environmental impacts of food production, fueling preferences for animal welfare, organic foods, environmentally friendly farming practices, and foods with a low "carbon footprint."[4] Farmers, processors, and retailers that respond to these concerns can expand their market share.

Comparable trends in the Western Balkans are limited to specific population segments in main cities where incomes have risen significantly. But as economies develop and incomes increase for more households, consumer behavior and food markets will see trends similar to those in Western Europe. Retailers are preemptively responding by introducing private standards that are more stringent than public standards (see below). Not responding to changing consumer demands will exclude local producers, who are in a unique position to take advantage of both high-value export markets and low-cost domestic markets, from a lucrative, rapidly growing quality segment.

Markets Are Liberalizing

While consumer preferences are changing, economies in the Western Balkans are opening up, exposing their markets to competition from high-quality, low-cost imports. The EU is the region's biggest trading partner, trading €79 billion with South Eastern Europe in 2005, up 53 percent from 2001. Trade agreements between the countries of the Western Balkans and the EU provide access to high-value EU markets for agricultural and food products. But these agreements also open the Western Balkans to more food imports from the EU, raising the pressure on farmers and processors to become more competitive.[5] Tellingly, although the increase in food exports to the EU was experienced by all countries in the region, the largest increases were recorded by Romania (67 percent) and Bulgaria (52 percent), aided by their improved standards during the EU pre-accession process.[6] Producers who cannot compete will be excluded from more lucrative, quality-oriented market segments and limited to traditional market outlets that are highly sensitive to regional economic fluctuations.

Compliance with EU Food Quality and Safety Standards Is Also Important

Although increasingly driven by consumer preferences and the retail sector, thus far food safety in the Western Balkans has been driven more by stringent food quality and safety standards in line with EU regulations. For example, EU Regulation 852/2004 involves implementing hazard analysis and critical control point (HACCP) principles for each operator in the food chain. For primary production, this means practicing good hygiene. In the dairy sector, this means maintaining the cold chain for food that cannot be stored at ambient temperatures; complying with microbiological criteria and temperature control requirements; conducting sampling and analysis; keeping records; optimizing layout, design, and construction of food premises; and monitoring foodstuffs transport. EU Regulation 853/2004 outlines specific hygiene rules for food of animal origin—for example, covering raw milk requirements for primary producers—and packaging and labeling requirements. Noncompliance with these regulations will act as a trade barrier to the EU market.

Investment in the Retail Sector Is Increasing

The food retail sector in Central and Eastern Europe, particularly in the Czech Republic, Hungary and Poland, has seen consolidation, rise of the large-scale retail sector, and entry of multinational corporations.[7] Although the sector is still developing in the Western Balkans, investment, consolidation, sales, and cross-border transactions have all been increasing (figure 2.1). Retail markets in the Western Balkans are dominated today by local retail groups that have started a consolidation wave.[8] Mergers and acquisitions are growing, and the retail market is expected to become increasingly concentrated.[9]

The dominance of regional players in the Western Balkans contrasts with Central and Eastern Europe, which has seen investment from the main Western European retailers. This is due in part to historically strong local agricultural groups in the Western Balkans and to Western European retailers' focus on the higher income markets of Central and Eastern Europe.[10] The relatively lower income markets of the Western Balkans are expected to continue to be dominated by regional players for some time.[11]

What Changes Are Occurring in Food Value Chains?

Modern retailing is fundamentally changing the technical infrastructure and entrepreneurial behavior in the agri-food systems of the Western

Figure 2.1. The Modern Food Retail Sector Is Growing Rapidly

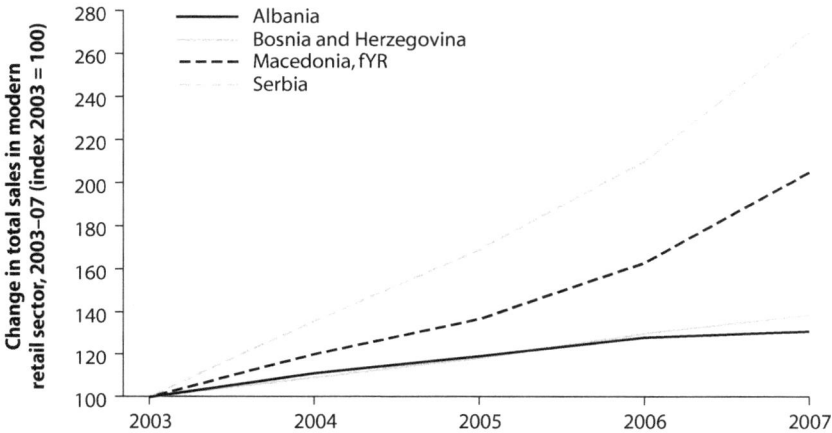

Source: PlanetRetail Database 2007. Data for Montenegro not available.

Note: The modern retail sector or "modern grocery distribution" includes hypermarkets, superstores, supermarkets, discount stores, convenience stores, drugstores, and cash-and-carry. It excludes independent specialist outlets such as butchers, bakers, and open markets. Grocery products include food and nonfood items when sold by mixed retail formats.

Balkans, with their currently complex and highly fragmented production systems and small-scale, unorganized producers with less sophisticated production structures and quality control systems.

Although value chain integration is driven by consumer demand, the actual process of integration is led by downstream segments—that is, food retailers and agro-processors. Local producers will have to comply with more requirements on product quality, consistency, and traceability from large food retailers. These requirements are often more stringent than and different from local standards in domestic markets. By not complying, local producers risk being excluded from this growing market segment.

To boost competitiveness, businesses have two strategies: cost leadership (low price) and differentiation through increased value added (high quality). Both strategies require better vertical coordination and logistics in the food chain. To reduce costs, businesses need to cut the costs of transactions as a product moves through the chain. To improve quality, they must coordinate product handling at different stages. This section looks at how retailers are responding to opportunities created by changing demand and how their responses are transforming the rest of the value chain.

Restructuring and Private Standards Are Driving Changes in the Food Chain

Stringent retailer demands on quality, consistency, and traceability mean that agri-food businesses must better coordinate production and logistics. The two most influential developments are the restructuring of retailer procurement practices and the increase in private standards on quality, volume, and consistency. Restructuring involves more retailer-processor and retailer-producer coordination and tends to have two stages.[12] First, retailers shift to centralized—and then cross-border—procurement, which favors high volume, coordinated deliveries from suppliers. Second, retailers develop a preference for specialized (in one or a few product categories) and dedicated (to supplying to the supermarket sector) wholesalers. They also use international logistics firms to coordinate logistics through the chain. Suppliers that can provide the desired product consistently and in sufficient volume become preferred suppliers; suppliers that cannot may find it harder to penetrate the modern retail channel. Retailers set their own standards for food quality and safety that can be stricter than public standards. Producers who do not meet private standards will not have access to retailers' markets, even though they may meet public standards (box 2.1).

Box 2.1

Producers That Stay Ahead of the Curve Have a Competitive Advantage

Producers that make early investments in food safety and preempt consumer preferences for safe products can seize the advantage from their competitors, even if the standards that they achieve go above and beyond what is required by public and retailer standards. One U.S. meat processing plant used innovative technology to produce safer meat for hamburgers. Although the final product costs up to 25 percent more than that produced by competitors, the firm has an important market share, with its meat found in 75 percent of hamburgers sold in the United States. Restaurants and retailers are willing to pay the difference as a result of several past food scares associated with hamburgers. The firm's sterile production methods are also more efficient, permitting its plant to operate nonstop.

Source: Washington Post 2008b.

Croatia's fresh fruit and vegetable value chain illustrates the impact of retail sector developments on primary producers and the value chain.[13] In the second half of the 1990s, Croatian retail chains bought most of their fresh fruits and vegetables from informal truck markets. The first step of restructuring the value chain was to procure more fruits and vegetables from dedicated wholesalers, who then started outgrower schemes to ensure quality and consistent supply and increased their imports of fresh fruit and vegetables. Retailers eventually moved away from wholesalers and established their own outgrower schemes, managed through holding companies, and selected preferred suppliers from outside the outgrower schemes. With the retailer directly connected to the outgrower, the value chain is more efficient, and traceability is enhanced.

Value Chains are Adapting

The effects of more rigorous food quality standards on the value chain, whether from private or public standards, can be seen in a number of cases. Case studies illustrate how value chains are integrating and consolidating—for example through better information flows, changing product collection practices, or innovative contract arrangements between value chain segments. They also demonstrate how downstream segments of the value chain—retailers and processors—are leading coordination. These case studies are not intended to be seen as models for value chain development—rather they illustrate the factors and practices driving value chain development.

Montenegro's dairy sector

Montenegro's dairy sector is typical of the fragmented value chains discussed in chapter 1.[14] Production is centered on small family farms with a small herd (two to three cows) and low annual milk productivity (2,000 kilograms per cow). Less than 15 percent of milk is delivered to the dairy processing sector, which is also very fragmented; most dairy processors collect milk directly from farms, even from small farms that produce very small quantities and do not have cooling tanks. Collection stations are much less common than in Bulgaria and Romania, making collection time-consuming and limiting how far dairy processors can be located from farms. Vertical integration between dairy farms and processors is also limited.

The challenges facing the Montenegrin dairy sector mimic those faced by Poland's dairy processors, which prior to EU accession had to stop accepting lower quality milk from suppliers to comply with the *acquis*.[15] Ensuring quality requires investing in a cooling tank for milk to maintain the cold chain, but small dairy farmers often cannot afford their own cooling tank. One solution lies in horizontal integration (links between farmers)—for example, joint use of a cooling tank by a number of small farmers. Dairy processors in Poland provided cooling tanks to the collection stations where they bought milk, which improved the quality of the milk collected.[16]

The Western Balkans has had some success in upgrading milk quality. Most milk meeting EU standards (extra and first class milk) comes from Croatia, where 50 percent met EU standards in 2005, up from 31 percent in 2003. Other countries are lagging behind; in Serbia, for example, only about 10 percent of milk meets EU standards. The main obstacle, as in Poland, is very small dairy farms, which raise collection costs and make it harder to improve milk quality.

To better compete, Montenegrin dairy processors must be able to collect more high-quality milk. Restructuring at the farm level and improving vertical and horizontal coordination are two methods. As in Poland, several processors are investing at the farm level to increase herd size and improve equipment. Some efforts are aimed at larger farms, others at all farms. Some dairy processors supply feed to their farmers at below market cost, while others provide such benefits as free delivery or discounts for large feed orders to larger farms. One processor has helped farmers buy more productive cow breeds from the Netherlands; the farmers repay the credit over five years through deductions in their milk payments. This arrangement addresses two agricultural credit constraints: bank loans are often difficult for small dairy farms to obtain and come with higher interest rates. Investments are not always dairy-specific: one dairy processor offers credit lines to its suppliers to buy household appliances, while another provides farmers with cards for credit in retail outlets stocking the dairy's products (the dairy acts as a guarantor).

This example illustrates the efforts pursued by Montenegrin dairy processors to strengthen the production capacity of their milk suppliers and, to some extent, to encourage farm consolidation by favoring larger farms. It also highlights the financial costs borne by dairy processors, limiting their profitability. To limit the financial impact on dairy processors, the public sector could do more to strengthen rural credit and extension systems, focusing on farms with a commercial future. As in other regions of the world, cost-sharing through public grants—for example, through a competitive public grant scheme modeled after the EU IPARD program—could be used to cofinance investments in milk quality (such as cooling tanks and milk parlors).

fYR Macedonia's wine sector

Some 25,000 Macedonian farms are involved in viticulture and wine production, mainly small vine growers with an average of 1.1–1.3 hectares spread over several plots.[17] They typically sell grapes to fYR Macedonia's 49 small and medium-size wineries that process about 65 percent of all wine grapes, making the rest into domestically produced wine and brandy for their own consumption. Vertical integration used to be common among smaller wineries, many of which have their own vineyards. Larger wineries depended largely on independent growers, paid by weight of grapes rather than by quality. Much of the Macedonian wine production was sold in bulk at low cost to Germany. More recently producers have attempted to move up the value chain by selling higher value products. The U.S. Agency for International Development (USAID)'s Macedonia Competitiveness Activity project supported the wine industry by focusing on quality and marketing improvements to boost sales of high-end specialty wines in Europe. The largest wine company, Tikves, has significantly modernized production and restructured its product portfolio toward high premium-branded wines.

A crucial part of the project was to increase cooperation between growers and wineries to improve grape quality. In 2004 a model purchasing contract based on quality standards was developed and discussed with wineries and growers. One winery achieved modest success in 2004 with quality-based contracts with growers and signed more than 1,700 in 2005. Other wineries have followed suit—an important first step toward long-term cooperation between growers and wineries and improving wine quality. The project also promoted marketing departments in wineries, supported wineries' marketing in the EU, and produced studies of the Dutch, German, and U.K. export markets.

Attempts by the Macedonian wine sector to evolve toward higher quality, high-value-added markets, driven by foreign and local consumer preferences, shows that contract farming can sometimes improve vertical coordination along the value chain, in particular to introduce higher quality standards. The public sector can facilitate development of quality standards (that can be used as references in contracts), arbitration, and contract enforcement.

Serbia's sugar sector

Sugar beet is grown mostly in Serbia's northern Vojvodina province.[18] The area under sugar beet has increased rapidly from just over 40,000 hectares in 2000/01 to about 70,000 hectares in 2006/07. Serbia's sugar beet processing facilities are fully owned by international companies, and the sector is highly vertically coordinated, with annual contracts negotiated between growers and processors specifying issues such as pricing, quality, and payment arrangements and production. The processors provide prefinancing for inputs and collection and transport to processing plants and decide on the harvesting schedule, payment schedule, and barter terms.

Several models have been developed to facilitate producer access to expensive machinery such as tractors. In some cases the processor acts as a bank guarantee for the producer, thus securing more favorable credit conditions. Alternatively, the processor provides machinery to the farmer, who must pay for it over five years, either with cash or in-kind, or the processor leases a machine to a producer. In other cases several producers join together and buy the machine with their own funds, independent of the processor—a scenario becoming more common with more affordable secondhand machinery now available following sugar regime reform in the EU.

In this value chain, consolidation has already taken place at the industry level. As a result, vertical coordination is more structured, and financing schemes supporting investment at the farm level are more developed. However, this case also illustrates how value chain integration can have both negative and positive dimensions. Recent history has shown that Serbian sugar beet producers gained by organizing themselves—for example, through professional organizations—to defend their interests. Until recently, relations between the industry and its suppliers were characterized by poor prices and payment terms. The public sector can promote—through legislation and taxation—professional organizations in the agri-food sector to facilitate coordination between various players.

Future Trends for the Agri-food Sector

Becoming more competitive will require substantial change in the agri-food sector, including fewer and larger farms, fewer people living and working in rural areas, and a smaller role for agriculture in the economy. This section discusses what will happen to the sector, based on current trends and examples from countries that have gone through a similar shift.

The farm sector in the Western Balkans is expected to gradually consolidate, as it did in new EU member states with similar production structures. In Poland developments in dairy processing have been gradually transforming the farm sector.[19] The number of medium-size farms has dropped, with some expanding and others (mainly older farm households) shifting from commercially oriented to subsistence farming. Similarly, the share of larger farms (five or more cows) in Bulgaria's dairy sector has been increasing, while the number of smallest farms is falling.[20] The Hungarian dairy sector has also seen similar trends. In 2005 only 16,061 dairy farms remained, half the number in 2000.[21] Some 572 commercial dairy farms now have 70 percent of all dairy cows.[22]

The Western Balkan countries have already seen similar developments. In Serbia the number of milk suppliers declined from 165 in 2000 to 63 in 2006. The milk supply stayed constant over that period, but milk delivered to dairies increased from 553 million liters to 740 million liters. This consolidation is enforced by a number of private and public policies. Serbia's Imlek dairy buys milk exclusively from producers with a minimum volume of daily milk supply (20 liters), and Croatia's Vindija dairy offers price incentives for larger quantities of milk. On the policy side in Croatia, price premiums are available only to farms with at least five cows, while in Serbia four cows are needed to qualify for subsidized equipment purchases. These policies favor efficiency, but appropriate policies for smaller farms are still needed to ensure equity.

In agro-processing, as with primary production, complete privatization of *agrokombinats* and processing companies, as well as a gradual trend toward consolidation, are expected. In most sectors the smallest processing units will find it hard to operate with increasing competition from larger processing plants with foreign direct investment and from increased imports. Moreover, as policies align with EU food quality and safety standards, smaller processing units might find it difficult to comply with the rules and will be excluded from the market.

Eventually, producers who do not upgrade their skills and technology will be unable to compete and will be forced to abandon commercial production. But the decision to do so will also be a function of income opportunities in other sectors—highlighting the importance of providing farm households with education assets to take advantage of these opportunities. Until other sectors of the economy develop, a dual agri-food sector is likely to continue. A few better-equipped, commercially oriented producers and processors will adapt to the new framework (driven by market incentives and access to capital), and others will continue with (semi-)subsistence and informal markets. Governments will have to account for this socioeconomic parameter to avoid further impoverishing rural areas.

As value chain coordination gathers pace, productivity (yields) and quality improvements will substantially boost competitiveness. But agriculture's contribution to total GDP in the Western Balkans will decrease from today's 10–23 percent, a trend already under way as other sectors of the economy grow, to stabilize at Southern European levels of 5 percent or less in the long term.

As chapter 1 notes, the Western Balkan countries have 20–60 percent of their workforce employed in agriculture. This rate reflects considerable underemployment because of few opportunities outside the agri-food sector. As off-farm opportunities increase the percentage of the workforce in agriculture will decrease, probably ending up closer to the Southern European average of less than 15 percent.

The rural population accounts for about 45 percent of the total population in the Western Balkans, compared with 35 percent in Southern Europe. Demographic change is an important part of farm consolidation because it affects rural land use and ownership. It also brings to the fore rural space maintenance, which is becoming an important rationale for the CAP.

The rural and agri-food sector in the Western Balkans will likely move in the same direction as those in Central and Eastern Europe and Southern Europe. But how fast change occurs depends on the public policies in Western Balkan countries. Several factors can inhibit primary sector consolidation, including investment and access to credit, access to public services and quality infrastructure, and—most important—incentives for farmers and processors to make productivity-enhancing investments. For example, price-support measures in Bosnia and Herzegovina may increase land prices and hinder farm consolidation. Inheritance laws and lack of tax incentives for agricultural production may also restrict consolidation. Chapter 3 discusses how to create adequate nonfarm income opportunities through effective rural development programs, and chapter 6 discusses strategies to promote modernization.

Notes

1. "Value chains" are frequently referred to as "supply chains." The term "value chain" encompasses not only the physical delivery and logistics of getting the product from production to consumption, but also the value that can be created by actors at each step in the chain and how all the actors within the chain can become more efficient.

2. The main worries include pesticide residues in fresh fruits and vegetables and cereals (71 percent of respondents); unhygienic conditions in food handling

outside the home in food processing plants, restaurants, and the like (69 percent); residues such as antibiotics and hormones in meat (68 percent); new viruses such as avian influenza (66 percent); and contamination by bacteria such as salmonella or listeria. There are differences in the relative importance of these perceived risks across member states, but clearly food hygiene and safety are a priority for EU consumers (European Commission 2006d).

3. There is a difference here between new EU member states, where consumers emphasize enhancing rural areas, stabilizing agricultural markets, and protecting family-type farms, and older EU member states, where they emphasize environmental protection, animal welfare, and sustainability of production (European Commission 2007a).

4. Garside and others 2008.

5. In November 2001 the Western Balkan countries received preferential export status with the EU, exempting their products—including agricultural products except wine and some types of fish and baby beef—from EU import tariffs. Albania, Bosnia and Herzegovina, Bulgaria, Croatia, fYR Macedonia, Moldova, Romania, and Serbia and Montenegro established several bilateral free trade agreements under the framework of the Stability Pact for South Eastern Europe. Liberalization will occur gradually, and each country has excluded sensitive products from the agreement. The Central European Free Trade Agreement (CEFTA), comprising Bosnia and Herzegovina, Croatia, fYR Macedonia, Moldova, Montenegro, Serbia, and the United Nations Mission in Kosovo (on behalf of Kosovo), came into effect in 2007. It aims to establish a free trade area between the member states by December 31, 2010, and replaces the 32 bilateral free trade agreements in the region. Finally, Bosnia and Herzegovina, Montenegro, and Serbia are joining the World Trade Organization (WTO). A likely result will be a reduction in the relatively high tariff equivalents in force in these countries (an average of 22 percent in Serbia).

6. Agra Europe 2006.

7. Dries and others 2004.

8. Serbian Delta Holding and Croatian Agrokor, both retail conglomerates in their home countries, have started expanding into regional markets. Agrokor has opened new supermarkets in Serbia and in 2007 acquired a locally owned retailer in Bosnia and Herzegovina. In 2007 Delta acquired local retailers in Bulgaria and Bosnia and Herzegovina, and Slovenian retailer Mercator acquired Rodic, the second largest retailer in Serbia.

9. Delta had 63 percent of Serbia's retail market share in 2006, and Croatia's Konzum had 30 percent (PlanetRetail 2006).

10. Dries and others 2004 classify countries as first, second, and third wave based on the speed of modernization, consolidation, multinationalization, and the like in the retail sector. The Czech Republic and Hungary are considered

first-wave countries, having received Western European foreign investment in the local retail sector as early as the second half of the 1990s (some local retail chains had emerged after privatization of the state-owned system, but very few were able to stand their ground against the major foreign retailers). Croatia is considered a second-wave country, where investment lagged a few years. Serbia and other Western Balkan countries are considered third- (or fourth-) wave countries, with major foreign investors only marginally interested (but expected to start investing in the future). The longer it takes foreign retailers to enter the market, the longer local and regional retailers have to grow and secure market share. The existence of these strong local agricultural groups in the region has likely helped this regional growth (since they have the base and the means to make investments in their operations and expansion).

11. The local players that dominated the retail market are involved in a range of vertically and horizontally coordinated businesses, with retail just a limited part of their activities, making them unique in the European retail scene. For example, in addition to a retail division, Delta M Group is involved in agricultural production and wholesaling and importing, which have all benefited and complemented the retail chain by supplying the stores with fresh and manufactured products. Agrokor, in addition to retail, owns food and beverage production facilities (PlanetRetail 2006).

12. Dries and others 2004 found that food value chains in Central and Eastern Europe are restructured in this way thanks to modernization of the food retail sector.

13. Reardon and others 2003.

14. FAO 2007c. The study included interviews with government institutes, farm associations and dairy processors.

15. Dries and Swinnen 2004.

16. Dries and Swinnen 2004.

17. FAO 2007a.

18. FAO 2004.

19. The Polish dairy sector was highly fragmented, with 89 percent of dairy farms having less than five cows in 2001 (Dries and Swinnen 2004).

20. Dries and Noev 2006.

21. CEEC AGRI POLICY 2006b.

22. CEEC AGRI POLICY 2006b.

CHAPTER 3

Beyond Agriculture: Meeting the Rural Development Challenge

As explained in chapter 1, the countries of the Western Balkans must increase the competitiveness of the agri-food sector while finding alternative economic activities for surplus agricultural labor. But the rural and agri-food sectors are not yet ready for such balanced development. Viable full- or part-time alternative income opportunities are needed to prevent future generations of smallholder farmers who lack physical assets and education from being trapped in poverty because they cannot find alternative employment. Alternative income opportunities are also needed to prevent increases in inequality in rural areas as modernization of the agri-food sector sees land, machinery, and processing facilities concentrated among larger commercial farmers.

Part of the solution is to encourage nonfarm development in rural space. Governments that focus on more than the agri-food sector will help ensure equitable development of rural areas. This chapter highlights how diversified and knowledge-based rural economies can promote socioeconomic cohesion in the context of EU integration. It underlines the roles for national and local governments, rural communities, and the private sector in fostering comprehensive rural development, and highlights key policy interventions—many of which can be undertaken locally—to promote nonagricultural growth in rural areas.

Key Messages

- Diversified and knowledge-based rural economies that are closely integrated with regional urban networks are the best vehicle for self-sustained growth and employment opportunities in rural areas.
- A territorial approach to rural development and the empowerment of regional and local authorities, rural communities, and the private sector can help governments maximize the impact of public investments.
- Investment in quality rural infrastructure, adequate human capital, an enabling business environment, and land consolidation is key for diversified and knowledge-based rural economies.

The Rural Development Challenge

The agri-food sector must undergo major modernization to realize its full potential and maintain commercial viability in increasingly open and demanding markets. Farming will become less a less important part of the economy in rural areas, but will still provide important environmental, cultural, and social services of tremendous economic value, such as agri-tourism (box 3.1).

Box 3.1

Success in Rural Development—Diversifying Away from Agriculture

Northeastern Italy's Veneto region is a good example of EU producers diversifying away from pure agriculture. Rural households in the region have brought agri-tourism into farming operations while emphasizing high-value foods. The region includes approximately 15,000 individual farms, with an average farm size of only 4.5 hectares. Producers were forced to generate large per hectare returns to support one or more family members without off-farm employment. Unlike the traditional system of transporting agricultural products to off-farm markets, agri-tourism brings customers to the farm. Veneto farmers who include agri-tourism in their farming operations have discovered that tourists are prepared to spend large amounts of money on vacations in rural areas. In addition to meals consumed onsite, tourists purchase locally produced wines, prepared meats, cheeses, jellies and jams, honey, baked goods, and crafts. In most cases agricultural production remains the farm's primary activity and agri-tourism is a secondary activity that adds value and marketing opportunities to the farm's crops and livestock production.

Veneto farmers must obtain a license to participate in agri-tourism. Farm operators must have two years of farming experience (which is also necessary to receive government funding), complete 100 hours of training, and pass an oral exam. The training includes courses on law, farm management, financial accounting, hygiene and sanitation, transporting and processing food products, and hospitality and can be adapted to address specialty products such as wine, cheese, or fresh produce.

Of the 15,000 farms in the region, about 260 are operating as *agriturismos,* or registered farms where guests can take a farm holiday. Farmers provide one of three levels of guest services: self-service snacks and light meals, full-service meals, or farm holidays that include meals, sleeping accommodations, and recreational opportunities. Farms can also sell products to be consumed later. Because of a short growing season and less diverse production potential, high-altitude farms have lower requirements for on-farm and regional production. Many farmers provide full-service meals only on weekends because weekends are the most popular days for tourism. The farmer receives an immediate supply of cash, and the family can then devote weekdays to other farming activities. Recreational activities for farm holidays include hiking, horseback riding, exploring historical landmarks, wine-tasting classes, stomping grapes, and evening musical events. Statistics compiled by regional agri-tourism consortiums indicate that farm families generally host guests fewer than 160 days a year, in part to meet the labor demands for the rest of the farming operation.

A limiting factor in Veneto agri-tourism is the cost of remodeling buildings to accommodate guests. For example, one Veneto family converted a dairy barn into a building that houses the farm's cheese-making facility and sales area, a restaurant, and guest rooms. The dairy operation was moved to a nearby facility. Although the Italian government provides grants for these projects, demand greatly exceeds funding. Annual income from agri-tourism ranges from €50,000 to €270,000 (in addition to other farm-related income), so some farmers are able to recover their initial investment relatively quickly.

Over the past five years, agri-tourism in Italy has increased by 25 percent, thanks mostly to more farms offering overnight accommodations. As noted, farmers are encouraged to promote traditional culture, social customs, and foods. The emphasis on traditional foods is enormously attractive in Italy, where, as in the Western Balkans, eating and sharing meals have historically played an important social role. At the same time, linking agri-tourism to local production appeals to modern consumers interested in alternative and sustainable tourism options, more information about the origin of the foods they consume, environmental responsibility and animal welfare, and health and nutrition. Producers in Veneto appear to be responding to this demand by slowly moving away from conventional agricultural production.
Source: Clemens 2004.

As agri-food assets shift from semisubsistence smallholder farmers to commercial operators, rural households' dependence on the agri-food sector will fall. The associated increase in scale, productivity, and competitiveness of the agri-food sector is a necessary but not a sufficient condition for equitable development of rural space. To ensure equitable development, governments must encourage nonagricultural growth and employment for farmers that can not scale up operations or find employment on commercial farms. Encouraging balanced growth in rural areas can mitigate socioeconomic problems such as lagging regions and slums.

Promoting Diversified and Knowledge-Based Rural Economies

Diversified and knowledge-based rural economies—with the agri-food sector integrated into the broader rural economy, which is in turn closely linked to regional urban networks—are the best way to create a self-sustaining rural space in the Western Balkans. This includes the multifunctional role of the agri-food sector, supporting other sectors such as tourism, and presumes that rural areas offer important environmental, cultural, and social services that benefit societies as a whole, including maintenance of landscapes and provision of an attractive living environment for professionals in regional urban centers. It is the basis for agri-environmental and income diversification activities in current EU support programs for rural development under Pillar 2 of the CAP and the EU IPARD program.

Diversified and knowledge-based rural economies in the Western Balkans depend on several interrelated factors. At the macro level they demand coherent and progrowth macroeconomic policies, including an open trade and investment climate, a low tax burden, and flexible labor markets. At the regional and local levels they depend on key production factors such as quality rural infrastructure and a well-educated, adaptable, and entrepreneurial labor force that can satisfy the rural development agenda. Furthermore, they demand a local business environment conducive to entrepreneurship, investment, and innovation.

Meeting these demands requires more than just increased budgetary resources for investment in rural development (see chapter 6). It requires adequate design and targeting of a broad range of public policies and investments. This section highlights how a territorial approach to rural development that includes empowering regional and local authorities, rural communities, and the private sector to define and leverage their economic potential can help governments of the Western Balkans meet the rural development challenge. In addition, it explains the role of quality rural infrastructure and human capital, an enabling business environment, and land consolidation in promoting a vibrant rural space.

Shifting to a Territorial Development Approach

Promoting broad-based and self-sustaining development requires shifting from the current sector-based policies to a territorial approach. This approach integrates rural and urban activities in a territorial dimension, covering a regional economy with both agricultural and nonagricultural activities. The territorial boundaries do not necessarily correspond with existing administrative boundaries and can include several municipalities and one or more small or medium-size cities. Including several municipalities creates economies of scale. Small or medium-size cities can be growth poles for rural areas, generating important economic spillovers through markets, basic public and business services, knowledge, and technologies. Recent EU regional development plans have focused on growth poles as well as links between growth poles and surrounding areas.[1]

A territorial approach to rural development requires an institutional framework that allows proper identification, evaluation, and implementation of a comprehensive set of public policies and investments. For example, policymakers need to make informed decisions on difficult tradeoffs such as focusing investment on infrastructure, education and health programs, or the business environment as the most efficient and effective way to promote balanced and self-sustaining development. In this context, participation of regional and local authorities, rural communities, and the private sector is critical.

Empowering Regional and Local Authorities, Rural Communities, and the Private Sector

Actively involving regional and local authorities, rural communities, and the private sector has been key to the effectiveness of several EU rural development interventions.[2] By mobilizing regional and local actors in territorial development strategies and plans, governments can ensure that public investment is in tune with local potential and needs and that these actors take full ownership of them. This bottom-up approach is relatively new to the Western Balkans and will require a substantial change in administrative culture, given the region's history of central planning and top-down governance. In addition, legal and regulatory frameworks need to be adjusted so that regional and local authorities, rural communities, and the private sector can actively participate in the strategic planning and implementation of public investment. The administrative capacity of these actors must also be strengthened.

The Leader+ program, a horizontal rural development support measure for EU member states under Pillar 2 of the CAP and for EU candidate countries under the IPARD program, has successfully introduced a territorial approach to rural development in eligible countries. It has established public-private partnerships in rural areas—so-called Local Action Groups (LAGs)—to prepare integrated development strategies for territorial areas that do not necessarily correspond to existing administrative boundaries and occasionally cross national boundaries. The strategies are based on a common vision for long-term economic potential among public authorities, private actors, and community groups represented in the LAG. They often present innovations for valorizing local environmental, cultural, and social resources as key ingredients for a self-sustaining development dynamic.

The territorial development strategies form the basis for concrete project proposals submitted by the LAGs for EU cofinancing under available rural development measures under Pillar 2 of the CAP or the EU IPARD program. At implementation, the LAGs are responsible for managing funds. Although only a small share of EU rural development funds are allocated to the Leader+ program, it has had a disproportionately positive impact on improving living standards in rural areas. In addition, EU member states have developed their own similar programs with national funding.[3] And civil society networks such as the Partnership for Rural Europe have emerged to promote exchanges and partnerships in rural development in EU and accession countries.[4] To avoid repeating costly mistakes and to maximize the impact of territorial and community-driven approaches to rural development, lessons from other countries should be considered.

Learning from Peers

A territorial and community-driven approach to rural development is a continuous learning process. There is no universal model for successfully developing diversified and knowledge-based rural economies. But several key lessons can shape the process (box 3.2).

Adequate national rural development strategies and support programs require proper monitoring and evaluation mechanisms that take into account the important lessons from other countries' experiences with this approach. In particular, countries with comparable geographic and climatic conditions, and at a similar level of economic development as the countries of the Western Balkans, could provide useful guidance.

Box 3.2

Lessons from Territorial and Community-Driven Approaches to Rural Development

- Territorial investments must reach a sufficient scale to generate spillover effects that unleash local, self-sustaining growth.
- Decentralized administrative functions must be accompanied by fiscal decentralization to keep regional and local decision-making from being overly dependent on central government allocations.
- Regional and local governments must have sufficient administrative and managerial capacity to prepare and implement complex territorial development plans.
- Bringing together rural and urban areas into territorial development requires that mutual benefits be clearly identified and advertised.
- Producers and civil society organizations must be promoted to ensure that different rural interests can be properly represented.
- Deep local inequalities may lead to the capture of benefits by local elites that reproduce social inequalities.

Source: De Janvry and Sadoulet 2007.

For example, while Ireland is often cited as one of the most successful examples of rural development in Europe over the last decade, it has geographic and climatic conditions that are much different from those in the Western Balkans. A better example may be regions in Italy such as Tuscany or Umbria, which have similar landscapes and climate.

Investing in Rural Infrastructure

As highlighted in chapter 1, good logistics are key for growth and competitiveness in the agri-food sector. They depend on high-quality infrastructure—such as roads, water, electricity, and information and telecommunication services—which lowers production and distribution costs and connects commercial farmers to suppliers and consumers in domestic and regional markets. At the same time high-quality infrastructure stimulates nonagricultural business development and improves rural households' living standards by increasing access to amenities and social services, including health and education. Quality rural infrastructure thus forms the basis for rural income diversification and can limit rural-urban migration flows.

Although investment in infrastructure is essential for reducing the peripheral status of rural areas, it is not enough on its own to sustain off-farm growth and employment. Only when based on local demand and combined with other services such as education and a better business environment can improved infrastructure services promote long-term sustainable growth and competitiveness.[5] This is because investment in infrastructure typically has decreasing marginal returns. Its impact on growth is often limited, with a short-term spurt in growth and employment that fades shortly after completion.[6] Infrastructure services must thus be combined with knowledge and innovation by mobilizing human capital and creating an enabling business environment.

Building Adequate Human Capital

Knowledge and good health promote labor productivity and reduce inequality. As noted in chapter 1, rural households in the Western Balkan countries have consistently higher poverty rates and lower education outcomes than do urban households. Investment in human capital is needed to close the poverty gap and enable rural households to escape the poverty trap. Rural households with more education tend to generate a larger share of income off the farm.[7] A healthy, well-educated, and adaptable rural labor force may find self-employment outside the agri-food sector and attract investment in higher-skilled nonfarm jobs less vulnerable to low-wage competition. In addition, with the relevant education and skills, residents of rural areas—in particular rural youth—stand a better chance of participating in urban labor markets, which typically provide higher wages.

Plenty of scope remains for improving education systems in the Western Balkan countries (table 3.1). The number of primary and secondary schools and qualified teachers in rural areas is often insufficient, schools are characterized by unsuitable curricula and lack of adequate learning tools, and dropout rates are often high. Given the long gestation for education investments to bear fruit, access to and quality of all levels of education—from primary to tertiary—must be expanded immediately. And curricula must be aligned with the skills required to contribute to rural development and successfully participate in urban labor markets. The rate of return on investment is estimated at 19 percent for primary education, 13 percent for secondary education, and 11 percent for tertiary education, although rates are slightly lower in non-OECD countries of Europe.[8]

Particular focus should go to secondary and tertiary education, which does not provide sufficient graduates with the skills for entrepreneurship and effective knowledge absorption and innovation. Public spending

Table 3.1. Global Competitiveness Index Rankings, 2007–08

Country	Overall ranking	Higher education and training ranking	Technological readiness ranking	Innovation ranking
Albania	109	103	74	131
Bosnia and Herzegovina	106	98	110	121
Macedonia, fYR	94	75	90	92
Serbia	91	82	57	78
Montenegro	82	79	48	104
Western Balkans average	96	87	76	105
Greece	65	39	58	63
Italy	46	36	27	47
Portugal	40	34	31	33
Slovenia	39	24	29	30
Spain	29	31	28	39

Source: World Economic Forum 2008.
Note: Lower ranking indicates more competitiveness. Rankings are out of 131 countries.

should be restructured to performance-based funding systems for educational institutions to provide incentives for enhancing competitiveness and providing opportunities. Public subsidies for fees could be targeted to students from poor households and linked to student loan systems.[9] Chapter 7 further discusses the needs of agricultural education, including at the tertiary level, in the Western Balkan countries.

Vocational training programs are also important. They should be tailored more to the needs of a rural economy based on income diversification, knowledge, and innovation. New skills needed include business management, marketing, environmental and natural resource management, and other topics that allow more rural residents to join the off-farm labor market and to establish businesses and services in rural areas.

Conditional cash transfer programs are another promising approach to improving human capital. As part of rural development support to noncommercial farm households, transfers could be linked to participation in educational programs, including vocational training programs. This could be an effective way to increase knowledge and skills in rural areas and to provide opportunities for the rural poor to educate their children. Programs of this type have been common in Latin America (Progresa in Mexico, Bolsa Escola in Brazil), with positive results.[10]

Research and development systems must also be improved to serve the rural development agenda. In the short run emphasis should be on adapting existing knowledge rather than on innovation. This requires stronger links between universities and enterprises in rural areas, which can help companies introduce new ideas and technologies. Focusing on applied research will also ultimately improve basic research. An efficient way for governments to do this is to work with the private sector to identify the strategic areas for investment in basic research, since private sector firms are better placed to identify commercial opportunities. Coordinated investment and shared resources (people, equipment, and ideas) between countries and institutions would increase economies of scale. Chapter 7 further discusses the role of agricultural research and development systems.

Creating an Enabling Business Environment

An attractive tax regime, the ability to start and expand nonfarm enterprises, to seek strategic business alliances, and to exploit synergies in line with current and future market demands are key components for sustained nonfarm growth and employment in rural areas. The Western Balkan countries face several constraints to a business environment conducive to diversified and knowledge-based development in rural areas. They include relatively high effective tax rates, limited access to finance, inefficient business registration systems, and inadequate legislation and regulation for protecting quality labels and geographic indications, and facilitating the formation of business partnerships and professional associations.

Taxation. An attractive tax regime is central for establishing incentives to start and expand businesses in rural areas and to create jobs. Corporate tax rates in the Western Balkans have dropped significantly in recent years. Albania, Bosnia and Herzegovina, and fYR Macedonia reduced their rates to 10 percent in 2007/08.[11] Personal income tax levels, which have a significant impact on small family businesses, are generally low as well. Macedonia (fYR) and Serbia recently introduced a flat rate (14 percent and 10 percent, respectively).[12] But the impact of these relatively low levels of corporate and personal income taxes is largely offset by a series of other taxes and fees, in particular social security contributions and high compliance costs.[13] In addition, value-added tax reimbursement time often exceeds the established deadline, and tax reconciliation is cumbersome.[14] Governments in the Western Balkans could address these constraints by reviewing tax compliance costs for small businesses, introducing mechanisms for identifying and tracking value-added tax reimbursements systematically, and allowing greater flexibility in tax reconciliation.[15]

Access to Finance. High interest rates are a frequently cited constraint to growth in rural areas in the Western Balkans. Although better access to finance through subsidized credit lines is often proposed as a solution, it does not address the underlying reasons for high interest rates. Rates can be high either because there is not enough liquidity in the credit market or because costs (risks) of investments are very high. In general, credit liquidity in the Western Balkans is not a problem. Local (and foreign) banks have enough resources to lend to worthy creditors, but they consider the risk of investing in rural areas high for a multitude of reasons—and thus charge higher interest rates. Remote rural areas make loans expensive to monitor, and land—a potentially important source of collateral—is not readily traded or properly valued. A more sustainable strategy to address these underlying issues could include improving land market administration, offering banks incentives to open branches in rural areas, and training loan officers how to properly evaluate loan applications from rural areas.

Business Registration. One of the simplest ways for local governments to contribute to broad-based rural development is to simplify procedures for setting up a business, thus enabling local entrepreneurs to take advantage of new business opportunities. As already indicated in chapter 1, despite significant variation across the Western Balkans, it takes 27 days, 10 procedures, and 21 percent of per capita income to start a new business in an average Western Balkan city. A city with this performance would rank 114 when compared with the 178 representative cities worldwide and roughly match the overall performance of Kenya.[16]

Several relatively inexpensive measures could improve the overall business registration process. For example, governments could eliminate operating or utilization permits and instead adopt a self-compliance principle. They could abolish minimum capital requirements and introduce one-stop shops (recently introduced in Albania and fYR Macedonia) for business startups, make registration electronic, standardize incorporation documents, publish application instructions, and eliminate antiquated requirements such as company seals or stamps. In addition, governments could authorize local offices of business registries to perform all the functions that can be carried out in the capital.[17]

Protection of Quality Labels and Geographic Indications. For rural areas to realize their full economic potential, they must make the most out of all their assets. The Western Balkan countries are endowed not only with high-value environmental and cultural assets such as scenic landscapes, national parks, and historical towns, but also with the quality and reputation of agricultural products specific to certain areas (including wine, cheese, ham, and spirits). Rural areas in the Western Balkans could benefit substantially from a legal and regulatory framework that effectively protects quality labels and labels of origin based on geographic indication. When combined with rural development programs associated with recognition and promotion of these labels—for example, through the development of agri-tourism—governments could help rural residents capture more of the value of their amenities.

Realizing this potential requires better agri-food product standards and certification systems and capacity building for producers and processors. It also requires stricter enforcement of food safety and other public standards—that is, less tolerance for informal value chains—to improve the chances of producers and processors that opt for higher standards (see also chapter 4). At the legal and institutional level, implementing labels of origin and quality requires a framework for recognizing the specifications. For geographic indications, specifications—including the delimitation of area—are proposed by the private sector's promoters of the origin-based product and must be recognized by public authorities that will protect them under intellectual property rights. In addition, certification is necessary to ensure that products conform to specifications. Traceability and control procedures also have to be included.[18]

Business Partnerships and Professional Associations. As chapter 2 highlights, one driver of a competitive agri-food sector is modern value chains, which maximize efficiency of production. Their development is equally important for non-agri-food sectors. In this context, business partnerships and professional associations are crucial for allowing greater vertical and horizontal economies of scale in the value chain. They are also a precondition for a stronger and more effective representation of farm and nonfarm interests in different segments of value chains and in any policy dialogue with governments.

Horizontal and vertical value chain integration and the formation of interest groups can work only with private initiative, but governments can support the process by establishing a legal and fiscal framework that favors business partnerships and professional organizations and encourages various actors in value chains.

Supporting Land Consolidation

Land consolidation and rural development go hand in hand. As noted in chapter 1, one of the biggest obstacles to a modernized agri-food sector and a vibrant rural space in the Western Balkans is the dominance of many small and fragmented semisubsistence farms. Development of commercially viable farms by consolidating available agricultural land resources is critical for the sector's future. The pace of consolidation will depend largely on nonfarm income opportunities for smallholder farmers whose agricultural assets are absorbed by commercial farms. Governments in the Western Balkans can further facilitate the process by promoting well-functioning land and rural property markets and by improving land-use planning. These efforts should also include developing capacity for implementing current and future EU support programs for agriculture and rural development.

To promote well-functioning land and rural property markets, including leasing markets, governments in the Western Balkans will have to ensure up-to-date land registration and nationwide cadastral systems. The countries of the former Yugoslavia have implemented projects to restore, modernize, and update land registration and cadastre systems, and Albania has created a completely new land registration system, but these efforts are incomplete.[19] Land and rural property markets by themselves are not enough to promote consolidation of agricultural land. To be effective, voluntary or compulsory land consolidation programs are also needed. Land banks could help by making public lands available and by buying and selling privately owned agricultural land (box 3.3).

Box 3.3

Slovenia's Land Reserve Fund: How a Land Bank Works

Slovenia's Land Reserve Fund promotes land consolidation through sale and lease. It is made up of state land not yet restituted to its previous owners. In areas where land ownership patterns are complex, small units remain state property until a buyer comes forward. Where restitution has resulted in fragmentation of a larger land unit, the fund purchases the small piece from the new owner if the new owner desires. The fund then adds the land to its own stock, thus preserving a larger continuous unit. The fund also buys odd-shaped parcels, parcels difficult to access, and even land adjacent to an existing farm, at the request of the farmer, for lease back to that farmer. Agricultural land still owned by the state and unused land are thus the foundation of the fund. Farmers wishing to consolidate their land holdings contribute and withdraw land from the fund.

Source: Dimitrova 2004.

Rural property taxation, including taxes on agricultural land, is another policy tool to stimulate land and rural property markets and is also underused as a source of revenue in Western Balkan countries compared with EU members, especially for local governments. Rural property taxation serves principally to raise revenue for governments to deliver public services, but it can also persuade owners to sell unutilized land. The rural property tax systems in the Western Balkans, however, are not based on the market value of land[20] and are poorly enforced. In fYR Macedonia, for example, agricultural land is exempt from taxation if used for agricultural production,[21] but in reality this becomes a general waiver for tax on agricultural land. Combined with very low lease payment collection for state-owned land, this brings the cost of using state-owned agricultural land close to zero. Such tax breaks and low payment collection remove an important incentive for productive use of land and impede the private market.[22] At the same time, they are a missed opportunity to generate resources that support investment in rural development.

Public sector support schemes to farmers could also be used to encourage land consolidation (box 3.4). For example, investment programs such as the EU IPARD program could be made available only to farms larger than one hectare, thus encouraging consolidation of smaller plots to secure public investment financing. Such programs often have a ceiling as

---

Box 3.4

Promoting Land Consolidation through Agricultural Support Schemes in Croatia

Croatia provides an example of how an agricultural support system can be designed to encourage land consolidation. In 2003 two categories of farms were distinguished—commercial farms and noncommercial farms (semisubsistence and subsistence farms)—and support to the sector was divided into four types—direct payments, investment support, income support, and rural development schemes. Commercial farms are eligible for direct payments, investment support, and rural development schemes; noncommercial farms are eligible for income support and rural development schemes. The income support scheme is socially driven and not linked to production. Once a family farm applies for the income support, it declares itself noncommercial and becomes ineligible for schemes targeting commercial farms.

well, to avoid supporting very large commercial farms. Naturally, smaller farms must also be given access to public resources, but these need not be tied to farm size. Other compatible measures could be introduced to encourage transfer of land to more dynamic farmers, including support for early retirement and support to young farmers.

Governments in the Western Balkans could also improve the management of state-owned land to promote land consolidation, allowing it to be sold or leased in a way that improves rural land ownership structures. In Bosnia and Herzegovina, fYR Macedonia, and Serbia, some 10–20 percent of agricultural land is either still in state ownership or owned by former collective farms. Much of this land is not farmed or is used inefficiently, and the rights of former users are murky. Bosnia and Herzegovina, for example, still lacks a state-level restitution law. A clear policy must be articulated and ownership rights established. If the land is not privatized, it should be managed transparently and fairly.[23] Once land rights are clarified, the land could be part of a land fund used for consolidation efforts (see also box 3.3). This is beginning to occur in Lithuania, for example, where the Provisional Law on Acquisition of Agricultural Land foresees support for acquiring agricultural land to carry out land consolidation, create rational land tenure, and stimulate the development of land and rural property markets.[24]

In addition to well-functioning land and rural property markets, improvements to land-use planning in the Western Balkans are equally critical to support commercial farms and nonfarm activities in rural areas. However, land-use planning and rural spatial planning (territorial planning, regional planning, community area development planning) have been largely neglected. Illegal land development is a problem throughout the region, and land-use legislation tends to be over-regulatory, with little provision for local participation. Legislation in Bosnia and Herzegovina heavily regulates agricultural land use, while municipal land-use planning is carried out according to master plans prepared at the entity or canton level.[25] In Montenegro, preserving agricultural land and improving the structure and use of fertile lowlands are urgent problems.[26] Serbia still lacks a comprehensive spatial and land-use plan,[27] and fYR Macedonia's Ministry of Agriculture, Forestry, and Water Economy is setting up a Land Directorate responsible for establishing and maintaining a register of land parcels and databases for state land and current users and lessees. As part of Western Balkan countries' preparation for EU accession, land-use planning will become more important, necessitating more efficient and usable regulations and rural spatial planning, and more effective monitoring and enforcement to ensure compliance.

The Western Balkan countries should maximize available EU pre-accession assistance to build capacity in all aspects of land administration and land-use planning, including land registration and cadastre, land-use regulation, property valuation and taxation, conveyancing, and land consolidation. In addition, they should develop information systems to manage current and future EU assistance programs for agriculture and rural development, including the IACS and Land Parcel Identification System (LPIS). The latter draws on information in the land registration and cadastre systems to manage payments to farmers under Pillar 1 (market support and direct payments) of the CAP. The information systems required to access and manage EU assistance for agriculture and rural development are discussed further in chapters 6 and 7. While the EU is unlikely to support entire national land consolidation programs, it may be able to cofinance some activities, such as planning and establishing land agencies, training staff, establishing information systems, and formulating regulatory frameworks.

Notes

1. World Bank 2007c.
2. World Bank 2007c.
3. World Bank 2007c.
4. For more details, see www.preparenetwork.org/web/index.php?pid=1
5. World Bank 2008d.
6. World Bank 2007c.
7. FAO and UNESCO IIEP 2003.
8. Psacharopoulos and Patrinos 2002.
9. World Bank 2008a.
10. Rawlings and Rubio 2005.
11. World Bank 2008g.
12. OECD 2007.
13. OECD 2007.
14. OECD 2007.
15. OECD 2007.
16. World Bank 2008c.
17. World Bank 2008c.

18. Possibilities include certification by an independent body recognized in the export market; self-monitoring by a local group of stakeholders (producers, local authorities, traders, and the like); monitoring by national authorities of all mentions, avoiding possible conflicts of interest; participatory guarantee systems based on the principle of social control and trust of producers (established particularly with regard to organic farming); and a full-fledged independent certification system, with certification bodies accredited by national authorities.

19. For example, in 2006 the World Bank started a land registration project to develop a secure and efficient real estate registration system in Bosnia and Herzegovina.

20. Land valuation is moving from an obsolete system based on soil quality (currently the practice in all Western Balkan countries except fYR Macedonia) and land area to a market-based approach. However, slow land markets and few land valuation professionals mean that property valuation has not progressed much.

21. 2003 Tax Code amendments.

22. Brown and Hepworth 2002.

23. In Estonia, Lithuania, and Poland the state continues to own much agricultural land, and its land leasing activities undercut the entire private lease market (Gerber and Giovarelli 2005).

24. Daugaliene 2004.

25. Without such plans, municipalities are entitled to take their own decisions, although in Republika Srpska they have to be approved by the Ministry of Agriculture, Forestry, and Water Management.

26. The 1992 Law on Agricultural Land regulates the protection, utilization, improvement, and reform of agricultural land as a natural resource of general interest (Government of the Republic of Montenegro 1992).

27. Marosan and Vasovic 2005.

CHAPTER 4

The Increasing Importance of Food Safety

Investment in safe food is critical for agri-food sector competitiveness. As chapter 2 shows, value chains are transforming in response to changing consumer preferences, increasing demand that foods meet minimum safety and quality requirements, and the availability of high-quality, low-cost imports. With trade liberalization and higher foreign investment in retail come new international competition, rapidly evolving value chains, and increased importance of food quality and safety. In addition to improving public health protection, effective food safety systems are needed to keep the agri-food sector competitive in domestic and external markets. Taking advantage of expanding trade opportunities requires governments of Western Balkan countries to improve food safety, veterinary and phytosanitary standards, and management systems, and to integrate control measures across food chains. At the same time the private sector needs to invest substantially in food safety control systems and infrastructure to meet EU requirements for food safety.

Reforming and modernizing food control systems involve updating and modernizing laws and regulations, institutional frameworks, trade regimes, and enterprise ownership. All the countries of the Western Balkans are engaged in wide-ranging reforms to bring national food safety systems into compliance with the EU food safety *acquis communautaire*. Despite significant progress, however, key constraints remain with respect to legislative and regulatory reform, institutional capacity, infrastructure, and control and enforcement, and remnants of the socialist system still have a profound effect on the region's food control infrastructure. This chapter considers the implications of effective food safety systems in the Western Balkan countries and outlines a strategic approach to the adoption of the EU food safety *acquis*.

Key Messages

- Effective food safety systems are a precondition for both a competitive agri-food sector and better protection of public health.
- Building EU-compliant food safety systems requires a gradual and differentiated approach. Priorities should be based on a careful assessment of national needs to develop a system that can evolve with EU requirements.
- Food safety legislation must be enforced to reduce foodborne diseases and create incentives for agri-food businesses to upgrade food safety control systems to EU standards. National programs should be developed that combine both financial and technical assistance for these businesses.
- Over-regulation and institutions that create significant budgetary pressure and undermine the private sector's competitive advantage must be avoided in favor of effective communication and coordination among relevant institutions and a clear division of responsibilities.
- Advantages of cross-border institutional streamlining and regional approaches to effective allocation of food-safety control resources should be exploited.

Effective Food Safety Systems Will Be More Important

Food safety and quality will become increasingly important for maintaining agri-food competitiveness and for improving public health conditions in the Western Balkans. This section looks at the reasons why.

Protecting Public Health

Effective national food safety systems are essential for the health and safety of domestic consumers. Foodborne diseases caused by microbiological contamination—*salmonella, listeria, campylobacter,* and *e. coli*—remain a major public health problem in the Western Balkans due to poor hygiene in production, processing, storage, distribution, retailing, and catering. Control measures and good practices are also required to prevent chemical hazards in foods. Structural changes must be set out in appropriate legislation, and better hygiene practices at food-handling establishments enforced by responsible inspection services. Public education and training are also needed. In Albania 55 of 61 retail market sites had permits from local authorities, but only 14 met basic hygiene and sanitary conditions;[1] some district permits are issued without adequate tests. Fraud in food production and trade is another concern, especially mislabeling of alcoholic beverages, soft drinks, milk and dairy products, and oils. Particularly prevalent in imported products through falsification of expiry dates, this has potentially costly consequences for public health.

Animal diseases spreading to consumers of animal products are also a risk to public health in the Western Balkans (box 4.1). Interventions are needed to control on-farm diseases and to ensure appropriate controls and treatment in slaughterhouses and processing facilities.

Maintaining Competitiveness

Food scares, including outbreaks of foodborne diseases, can cause substantial commercial losses for the agri-food sector (box 4.2).

Taking advantage of new trade opportunities will require agri-food producers to improve the quality and safety of their products to comply with stringent EU requirements. As chapter 2 discusses, international food safety and hygiene requirements could be a trade barrier for domestic producers and exporters in Western Balkan countries. The trade deficits shown in chapter 1 suggest that this may already be the case. Western Balkan countries struggle to comply with international food safety regulations and requirements under the WTO Agreement on the Application of Sanitary and Phytosanitary Measures. Although WTO membership has opened new opportunities for trade in agri-food products, weaknesses in national food control systems seriously limit this potential. Private sector challenges to comply with food safety and hygiene requirements are another obstacle; they also undermine competitiveness in domestic markets, where consumers are emphasizing food safety and quality.

Complying with the EU Food Safety Acquis

Food safety is important for EU accession. The European Commission has said that "in the area of food safety the candidates need to ensure coherent transposition, implementation and controls throughout the whole food chain."[2] The challenge is to bring food safety and quality standards in candidate and potential candidate countries up to current EU levels and to not tolerate any weakening in food control standards within an enlarged internal market (box 4.3).

Box 4.1

Brucellosis Is a Public Health Threat in the Western Balkans

Brucellosis, particularly prevalent in Albania, illustrates the importance of tackling animal diseases. Albania has a high incidence of brucellosis among humans, which is transmitted either through contact with animal tissue or through drinking contaminated milk or eating contaminated milk products (see figure). Infection caused mostly by *B. melitensis* in ruminants reached its highest levels between 1960 and 1965, then declined after control measures were introduced. In 1989 Albania was free of cattle brucellosis and had low prevalence (0.002 percent) in small ruminants. But after the political and economic changes of the 1990s the infection rate in animals grew, peaking in 2002, due to uncontrolled movement of animals, failure to observe sanitary and quarantine rules, poor technical education for farmers, and a limited budget for an eradication strategy.[1] A new strategy for brucellosis control was introduced in 2003 and is yielding positive results.[2] Nevertheless, recorded infection rates reach 10 percent in several regions, and the number of people affected is increasing, particularly in rural areas.

Brucellosis Is Increasing in the Western Balkans

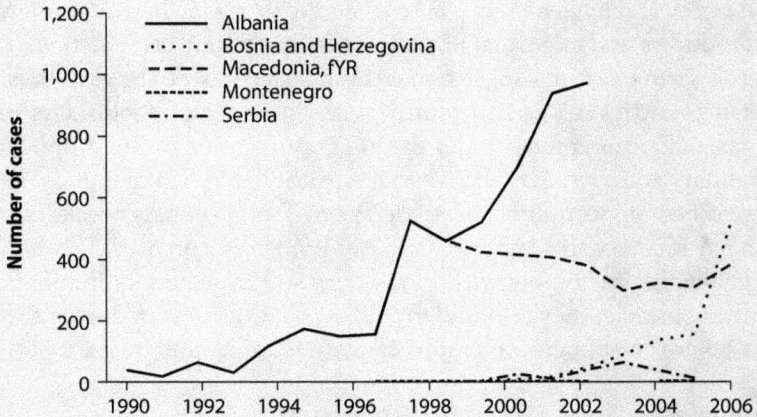

Source: Authors' communication with national public health authorities 2008.

1. Ministry of Health of Albania 2006.

2. The strategy involves vaccinating lambs and young goats (ages 3–6 months) in infective zones, extensively screening pregnant ewes using skin and serological testing, vaccinating female ewes 15 days after giving birth, eliminating positive heads within 15 days of their identification, and identification of vaccinated animals.

Box 4.2

Food Scares Can Devastate Agri-Food Business

The June 2008 outbreak of *salmonella* in the United States was originally linked to fresh tomatoes from Mexico, devastating Mexico's $900 million tomato industry, which sends 80 percent of its tomato exports to the United States. In the weeks following the outbreak exports stopped, and the price of a box of tomatoes dropped from $15 in the United States to $5 in Mexico, which became flooded with unexported tomatoes. But no link had been proven between the salmonella outbreak and Mexican tomatoes. The outbreak has since been attributed to jalapeño peppers, but the damage to the tomato industry has already been done.

Source: Washington Post 2008a.

Box 4.3

EU Food Safety *Acquis* and Enlargement: Maintaining the Integrity of the EU Food Supply

Food safety is a major challenge during the EU pre-accession process. Countries need to ensure coherent transposition, implementation, and controls throughout the food chain to ensure food safety. A high level of food safety across the EU is crucial for the internal market to function and for consumer confidence to be preserved.

The EU food safety *acquis*[1] covers numerous legislative acts that are often broad in scope and demanding in terms of transposition, implementation, and enforcement. It is therefore crucial that the *acquis* be fully transposed into national legislation and that administrative structures and procedures be strengthened and reformed before accession.

In addition to the efforts to comply with present EU requirements, countries need to take into account that the EU food safety *acquis* is fast-moving and often-changing. Western Balkan countries should thus focus on developing a food control system that can evolve, with a view to attaining EU standards in order to integrate existing structures and resources in an efficient organization.

1. Regulations of the *acquis* concerning the quality and safety of foods are found mainly in negotiation chapters 1 (Free Movement of Goods) and 7 (Agriculture).

While the Western Balkan countries are at different points in the EU pre-accession process, all are aware of the trade opportunities and benefits of compliance with the EU food safety *acquis*. They are thus involved in a wide range of reforms to modernize and reform food control systems. Assisted by international donors, particularly the EU, the Western Balkan countries are planning to ensure that the *acquis* is fully transposed into national legislation and administrative structures and that strong procedures exist before accession.

Progress in Adopting the EU Food Safety *Acquis*

In modernizing food control systems, the Western Balkan countries need to take into account basic principles accepted globally and within the EU to build sound and effective food control systems. These include enforcing food laws for consumers; managing hazards along the entire food chain; reducing risk through good agricultural practices, good hygiene practices, and introduction of the HACCP system; establishing emergency procedures (such as product recall); developing science-based food control strategies and standards; facilitating stakeholders' cooperation and active participation; and self-control by the industry. More specific EU food safety standards include rules on hygiene and control, food additives, animal identification and registration, and animal feed.

Establishing an EU-Compliant Regulatory Framework for Food Safety

All countries have recently approved or are in the process of approving new food laws that incorporate the basic principles of the EU General Food Law. Adopting and implementing secondary legislation is also an important step toward alignment with the EU *acquis*. In addition to basic laws on food, most Western Balkan countries have introduced new veterinary laws and regulations—Serbia, for example, is developing new laws on veterinary matters, animal feedstuffs and animal welfare—demonstrating that a solid foundation is being established. But problems still exist in implementation and enforcement (see below). To this end, efforts on secondary legislation include rulebooks on such topics as food safety monitoring, additives in foodstuffs, and official controls. Work needs to continue, however, since it takes time to identify and eliminate gaps, overlaps, and inconsistencies. Some aspects of the former Yugoslav system are being applied in parallel with new harmonized procedures.

Substantial effort is needed to bring control structures in line with EU requirements. The EU *acquis* includes specific rules for enforcement and compliance assessment that Western Balkan countries are taking steps to meet. These include annual control plans outlining inspection targets for veterinary drug residues and pesticide residues. The plans for veterinary drug residues are routinely followed in fYR Macedonia and Serbia, while national pesticide residue monitoring plans are ready for adoption. Other countries are aware of the need to comply. In 2004 Bosnia and Herzegovina introduced legislation on a residue-monitoring plan for animal products according to EU rules. fYR Macedonia has taken the most significant steps to comply with the hygiene package, while Bosnia and Herzegovina has started to develop secondary legislation.[3]

The prevailing inspection, monitoring, and surveillance system under the *gosudarstvennyy standart* (GOST)—a mixture of technical prescriptions, quality parameters, agricultural health standards, and safety standards inherited from the Soviet Union—must be redesigned in a progressive manner by the Western Balkan countries. Most of the health and safety standards are implicit and not based on transparent scientific criteria. Food safety requirements are often less strict than those in the Codex Alimentarius (see below) and other international standards. GOST standards are an obstacle to market access because they are not recognized in market economies, and they reduce export competitiveness because they give producers little flexibility to follow market trends and consumer taste (that is, quality specifications are subject to regulatory control) and involve extensive inspections throughout production and trade channels.

Western Balkan countries should also support the work of the Codex Alimentarius Commission.[4] The significance of Codex standards has been heightened since the introduction of the WTO Agreement on the Application of Sanitary and Phytosanitary Measures, which encourages WTO members to base their national food safety measures on Codex standards. Efforts have been made to promote Codex standards as part of the EU harmonization process. When preparing EU legislation, EU institutions typically consult Codex work, including scientific advice from the joint FAO/WHO expert bodies. This trend is expected to continue because in 2002 the EU agreed to take into account international standards when developing and adapting food laws. In addition, the EU became the first member organization of the Codex Alimentarius Commission in 2003.[5] Effective EU contribution to Codex standards requires active participation of EU member states and countries in the greater European region.

All countries in the Western Balkans are members of the Codex Alimentarius Commission, with Bosnia and Herzegovina becoming the newest member in 2007.

Establishing an EU-Compliant Institutional Framework for Food Safety

The Western Balkan countries should aim for an integrated approach to food control, with overall coordination at the national level and institutional arrangements that maximize regional (cross-border) collaboration and communication. The current fragmentation and distribution of official food control competences among different ministries has resulted in a disjointed approach, inefficient use of limited physical and human resources, and lack of coordination and communication. The traditional division of labor between the agricultural and health sectors has proven to be inefficient for dealing with food safety outbreaks when close communication among enforcement agencies is required.

A preventive approach to food safety, with the government taking advisory, oversight, and enforcement roles, requires food control systems with clear responsibilities and mandates. Governments need to devise mechanisms and organizational arrangements that clearly separate risk management and risk assessment, and avoid duplication of inspections, ensure integration of control plans and laboratory activities, and achieve best use of limited resources. Different models to enhance national coordination appear in Western Balkan countries. Given the region's capacity constraints, a lighter institutional framework should be established to be scaled up as necessary in line with the EU accession process, since an onerous food control infrastructure will place budgetary pressure on governments and undermine the private sector's competitive advantage. Nevertheless, the infrastructure should be sufficiently adequate and effective to ensure public health protection and facilitate emerging agri-food businesses.

Part of EU pre-accession is the preparation of an effective National Strategy for Food Safety Control to enable governments to develop an integrated, coherent, effective, and dynamic food control system, and to set priorities for better protecting consumers and promoting national economic development. The strategy defines objectives and means to improve the institutional framework for food control as well as the essential individual components. Given the numerous opportunities for donor aid, including a range of EU pre-accession and partnership programs such as the Instrument for Pre-accession Assistance (IPA) and the Technical

Assistance Information Exchange Unit (TAIEX), it would also guide donor projects and ensure that the donor support aligns with existing national priorities.

Ensuring Adequate Institutional Capacity

Inspection Services. Better enforcement of existing legislation on inspection is essential. Most emphasis has so far been on harmonization with the EU *acquis*—to the detriment of adequate implementation and compliance. But the benefits of these new laws will not materialize without effective and consistent implementation and enforcement. Inconsistent enforcement of Albania's Law on Veterinary Service and Inspectorate, for example, allows illegal practices to continue and discourages private investment in a sustainable network of modern, better equipped slaughterhouses. The rise of brucellosis incidents in humans indicates a serious lack of meat and dairy controls (see box 4.1).[6] Infected animals are supposed to be eliminated, but lack of strict controls means that there is little information on how this happens. While enforcement of animal health laws requires additional funds to strengthen municipal veterinary services, revenue is also generated by issuing veterinary certificates.[7] Moreover, the competitiveness of producers who comply with the laws is increased because the superior quality of their products becomes more apparent.

Inspection procedures will have to shift from the current regulation-focused approach to an enforced self-regulatory approach. An enforced self-regulatory approach relies on risk-based inspections of the production processes at agri-food processing facilities (applying HACCP principles) rather than sampling and end-product laboratory testing. This ensures that resources are focused on the food products and businesses that pose the greatest public health risk. Enforcement agencies must develop annual control plans, with guidelines and general rules for inspections at the central and regional levels. Compliance with these plans is critical, and requested information must be adequately provided (such as elements for monitoring plans of veterinary residues, medicines, use of hormones, details of methods of analysis, and the like). As the implementation of HACCP systems becomes mandatory, inspection services will become more important. They will be responsible not only for assuring implementation but also for providing implementation guidelines and control of certification.

Stronger border inspection posts are also needed with improved animal and plant quarantine facilities and practices in line with international WTO Sanitary and Phytosanitary Agreement obligations and EU requirements. Widespread problems in Western Balkan countries include administrative red tape, corrupt practices, a multitude of border controls by different agencies and a lack of cooperation between authorities on both sides of common borders. In fYR Macedonia, however, the Ministries of Health, Agriculture, and Environment worked together to develop a system for integrated border management through a Community Assistance for Reconstruction Development and Stabilization (CARDS) project.[8]

More trust between the official inspection services and the private sector can help build public-private partnerships for developing and implementing food safety standards. Inspection services will have to provide advice and support to help the private sector comply in the most efficient manner, especially small and medium-size enterprises that lack expertise and resources. This requires a fundamental shift from a culture of policing in response to noncompliance or acute food safety problems toward one of educating and facilitating. One recent positive example is fYR Macedonia's sector-specific hygiene guides developed by food business associations and approved by the government.

Laboratories. The current state-run laboratory networks in the Western Balkans generally cannot support a modernized agri-food sector. There are no overall laboratory strategies for testing food safety, so organizations and laboratories compete for resources without any overarching organization and coordination. All the Western Balkan countries must work together to rationalize the existing laboratory structure, provide adequate public funding for laboratory checks to lower the cost of compliance for producers, and eliminate possible collusion through proper regulatory enforcement. Strengthening the laboratory structure in this manner also requires risk-based sampling and analysis plans (targeting high-risk foods and hazards) and food safety decisions based on the results of that analysis. Closer interaction between official food inspection activities and laboratory analysis support is necessary to this end.

Current laboratory testing capacity for food safety is inadequate. Laboratories use outdated equipment and methods, and staff are often unskilled and need retraining in modern analytical methods. In addition, budgets are insufficient, and collation and reporting of results to risk managers is limited. This leads to suboptimal use of results for risk prevention. In some cases, laboratories cannot use sophisticated equipment provided by international projects because of irregular electricity supply, lack of after-sales service, or lack of technical support for calibration and reference testing. In addition to these basic weaknesses within individual laboratories, there are problems of unclear and overlapping roles and responsibilities, and a general lack of cooperation and information exchange. The likelihood of most laboratories obtaining international accreditation thus appears remote.

Given the small size and limited resources of the Western Balkan countries, governments should take advantage of regional capacity where they lack analytical capacity. Unless a laboratory provides a service across the Western Balkans, the costs and infrastructure requirements to establish specific analysis facilities for certain parameters (such as dioxin) may be overwhelming. Collaboration through regional centers of excellence specializing in efficient and effective testing of selected parameters may be a more cost-efficient solution.

Implications for the Private Sector

Bringing agri-food businesses up to EU standards will be a major challenge for the private sector, requiring substantial investments. As discussed in chapter 2, many producers and processors are unlikely to meet the EU requirements for the infrastructure and organization of agri-food value chains. The competitiveness of Western Balkans agri-food businesses is further undermined by insufficient supply, high raw material prices, and low-quality locally processed products. Poor capacity utilization among large agri-food businesses coupled with low production volumes among small agri-food businesses have resulted in outdated or limited technologies, lack of investment, and high unit production costs. These problems are exacerbated by a lack of knowledge of government requirements and standards; inability to apply good hygiene and manufacturing practices and quality assurance schemes (including the HACCP system); poor marketing information; inadequate packaging and labeling; and continuing mistrust of the potential benefit of more formalized collaboration in businesses.

Governments in Western Balkan countries can negotiate special provisions with the EU that allow low-capacity firms to continue producing for the domestic market without fully complying with EU requirements. Experience from the new EU member states shows that only large agri-food companies could make the necessary upgrades, even with EU assistance programs providing financial support.[9] Some 1,000 food processing plants in new EU member states were granted a three-year transition period starting May 1, 2004. These businesses accounted for only 8 percent of food processing establishments in these countries. Many companies whose production accounted for only a small fraction of overall output had to close, either because they were too small or because their processing facilities were too outdated. High-risk sectors such as meat production and processing in new EU member states faced substantial problems complying with EU hygiene and veterinary requirements (box 4.4). If special provisions are negotiated for small and medium-size enterprises to continue supplying the domestic market, they should reflect a stepwise approach and be based on a proper risk assessment.

Governments in the Western Balkans should develop national programs combining both technical and financial assistance to gradually improve agri-food businesses, including competitive grants (in the context of the EU IPARD program; see chapter 6). This will raise final product quality and safety and boost competitiveness. Programs could use competitive grants (in the context of the EU IPARD program; see chapter 6). A sensible application of the HACCP system, including a sound foundation of good hygiene, should be adopted in a stepwise approach. It may be appropriate for good hygiene practices to be implemented first in some sectors. Experience has shown the need for a coherent and consistent government strategy to avoid sending confusing messages to agri-food businesses. This requires similar approaches by different inspection services and is especially important for smaller businesses, which do not have the financial resources to contract private consultants and thus rely more on government guidance and support. Without this guidance and support, uptake of good hygiene practices and HACCP may be disjointed. In this context the shortage of local expertise to assist agri-food businesses in implementing EU food safety requirements needs to be addressed; certification for ISO and HACCP standards is currently performed only by accredited foreign companies.

Implications for Public Policies and Investments

Governments in the Western Balkans should adopt a gradual and differentiated approach to developing EU-compliant food safety systems, carefully sequencing and prioritizing their efforts based on specific national needs and a careful assessment of associated costs, benefits, trade opportunities, and public health risks. After this needs assessment, national food safety control strategies should be prepared as a guide for future public policies and investments. A clear strategy on alignment with EU requirements boosts the possibility of success and enables the effective and sustainable implementation of international donor assistance, which may otherwise be devalued by subsequent changes in a nonconsolidated

Box 4.4

New EU Member States Offer Some Lessons for Western Balkan Countries

When Poland acceded to the EU in May 2004, only 19 percent of Polish meat businesses fully complied with EU hygiene and veterinary standards and were thus licensed to export to other EU markets. These firms were high-capacity enterprises, accounting for 65 percent of Poland's total meat production (see figure). Some 71 percent of Polish meat firms did not meet EU standards. With their low production capacity, they fall under the EU special provision for small-scale enterprises. Some 47 percent of Polish meat firms complied with simplified EU standards and were thus authorized to sell on the Polish national market only. The remaining 24 percent had the largest shortcomings in meeting EU standards. A special law was enacted just before accession allowing very low-capacity enterprises (producing less than 4 tons per week) to maintain production, selling their goods on the very local market (that is, directly to end consumers). Western Balkan countries could adopt a similar approach for their meat sectors, negotiating special provisions that allow low-capacity firms to continue producing for the domestic market, even without fully complying with EU requirements.

State of Compliance in Polish Meat Production and Processing

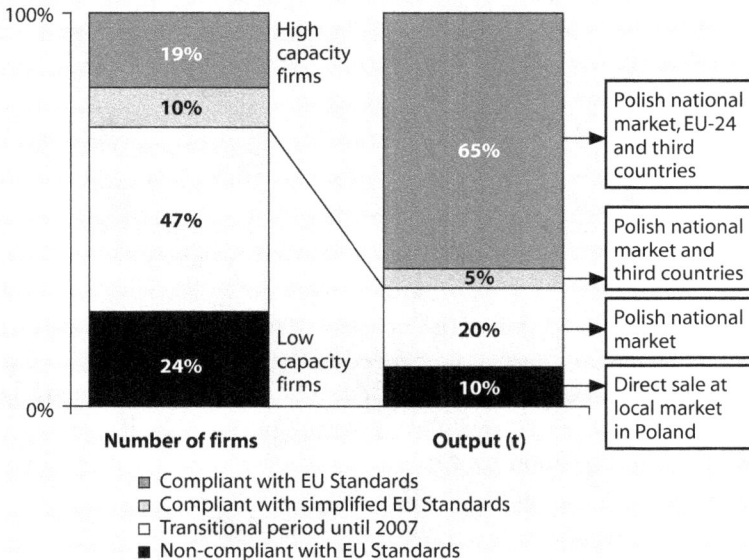

Legend:
- ▨ Compliant with EU Standards
- ☐ Compliant with simplified EU Standards
- ☐ Transitional period until 2007
- ■ Non-compliant with EU Standards

Source: Rau and van Tongeren 2006.

Note: Refers to slaughterhouses and processing enterprises of pork, beef, and veal, and poultry meat complying with Directive 64/433/EEC and 77/99/EEC.

system. The strategies would outline plans for transposing and implementing the EU food safety *acquis*, the institutional restructuring needed to establish an integrated approach to food control with overall coordination at the national level, and effective arrangements for regional (cross-border) collaboration and communication.

In preparing their strategies, governments should take into account that the EU *acquis* is a moving target. As a result, food safety systems will have to be able to evolve with changing EU requirements. In addition, they should provide for a gradual transposition and implementation of the EU *acquis* based on a broad consensus among stakeholders regarding market opportunities and major public health and commercial risks. Harmonization and enforcement of food legislation will be enhanced with the active participation of all parts of agri-food value chains. Governments must also stress the sound foundation of good hygiene practices, clearly state the primary food safety responsibilities of agri-food businesses, and underline the government's supportive role in helping the sector through adjustment.

Alignment with the EU *acquis* will require reorganizing and streamlining the existing institutional framework into an efficient organization for integrated food safety control, with overall coordination at the national level and clearly defined responsibilities for all involved agencies. Given current capacity constraints in Western Balkan countries, a lighter institutional framework is needed in the short run, to be scaled up during the EU pre-accession process. While the ultimate system will depend largely on current institutional arrangements in the food control system, food safety systems and measures will have to operate within a risk-analysis framework. This facilitates prioritization of risks to public health and the overall economy through assessments of real risks and enhances the best use of limited resources to control important food safety issues. Most Western Balkan countries have limited risk assessment functions, so stronger technical and human capacity will be needed in their veterinary, phytosanitary, and sanitary services. In addition, effectively enforcing food safety legislation will require more capacity in inspection services, in particular in relation to the transition to a risk-based inspection program, and ability to assess the application of good hygiene practices and the HACCP system by food businesses, and implementation of effective controls at border inspection posts. Testing facilities will also require major upgrades and modernization as well as a new focus suited to their new tasks. This effort will include a major consolidation of infrastructure and functions, which may be politically difficult.

Strong political awareness and commitment will be critical for successfully completing the alignment process. In particular, budgetary allocations for food safety control functions will need to be specified in the budgets of all government agencies involved in food safety control and be further broken down into official control (inspection and laboratory testing), reference laboratories, monitoring programs, risk assessment studies, border inspections, and the like. All actors should prepare annual plans and reports on their activities. And governments in the Western Balkans should pursue regional approaches to food safety—by assessing the usefulness and strength to be gained through regional initiatives, such as interlaboratory testing, regional training initiatives, cross-border issues, and harmonized food standards as a basis for interregional food trade. Such regional institutional streamlining is key to ensuring an effective allocation of food safety control resources and raising overall food safety and control of animal diseases.

Well targeted assistance will also be needed for the agri-food sector to adjust to increasingly demanding food safety standards. This assistance should come primarily in the form of competitive grants in the broader framework of rural development programs under the EU IPARD program (see also chapter 6). These programs should be accompanied by comprehensive training program for the private sector—for example in HACCP systems. In addition, academic institutions have to be built up to provide an educated workforce and research facilities that promote private food business innovation. Governments should adopt a pragmatic approach to compliance with EU food safety standards among small processors, which will find it difficult to make the necessary investments to meet the standards—for example, by negotiating special provisions for low-capacity firms to allow them to continue producing for the domestic market, even without fully complying with EU requirements (see box 4.4). As agri-food businesses expand and new businesses are established, however, new businesses should be held to a higher standard and forced to meet the EU minimum requirements.

Notes

1. UNECE 2002.

2. European Commission 2000.

3. The Hygiene Package includes the following EU Regulations/Directives: Regulation 852/2004 on the hygiene of foodstuffs (corrigendum published in Official Journal L 226) - general requirements primary production, technical

requirements, HACCP, registrations/approval of food businesses, national guides to good practice; Regulation 853/2004 laying down specific hygiene rules (corrigendum published in Official Journal L 226) - specific hygiene rules for food of animal origin (approval of establishments, health and identification marking, imports, food chain information); Regulation 854/2004 laying down specific rules for the organization of official controls on products of animal origin intended for human consumption (corrigendum published in Official Journal L 226) - detailed rules for the organization of official controls on products of animal origin (methods to verify compliance with Hygiene 1 & 2 and animal byproducts regulation 1774/2002); Directive 2002/99/EC laying down health rules governing the production, processing, distribution and importation of products of animal origin - veterinary certification, compliance with EU rules; and Directive 2004/41/EC repealing 17 existing Directives (corrigendum published in Official Journal L 195).

4. The Codex Alimentarius Commission was created in 1963 by the FAO and the World Health Organization (WHO) to develop food standards, guidelines, and related texts such as codes of practice under the Joint FAO/WHO Food Standards Programme. The program aims to protect consumer health, ensure fair trade practices in food trade, and promote coordination of all food standards work undertaken by international governmental and nongovernmental organizations.

5. The EU exercises its voting rights on an alternate basis with the member states according to their respective areas of competence.

6. This requires close cooperation among municipal veterinary services, road police, and border guards.

7. UNDP 2005 estimates a 6.7 million ALL revenue for the state veterinary service.

8. The Community Assistance for Reconstruction Development and Stabilization (CARDS) program was replaced by the IPA in 2007. Over 2000–06 the program had a budget of €4.65 billion to help the countries of the Western Balkans (Albania, Bosnia and Herzegovina, Croatia, fYR Macedonia, and Serbia and Montenegro) participate in the stabilization and association process and achieve close regional cooperation. Assistance was given to reconstruction and stabilization in the region; support for democracy, the rule of law, human rights, and minorities; economic development and market-economy-orientated reforms; and developing closer relations between the recipient countries and the EU.

9. For example, the EU's Special Accession Program for Agriculture and Rural Development (SAPARD) program assisted the agri-food sector in the new member states in adjusting to EU standards. The program focused in particular on improving the production/processing of agri-food products.

CHAPTER 5

Climate Change and Its Consequences

Investing early in climate change adaptations may produce large dividends for the agri-food sector. Scientists now agree that climate change is happening and that its impact is likely to intensify this century. According to the Intergovernmental Panel on Climate Change (IPCC), average annual temperature in Europe increased 0.9°C from 1901 to 2005—and will continue to rise.[1] The latest climate models project that the Western Balkans will become more subject to higher temperatures, reduced and more variable precipitation, and more frequent extreme climatic events, such as floods, droughts, and heat waves.

Climate change will create major challenges for agriculture. Heat stress and soil erosion will destabilize crop yields, and greater exposure to vector-borne pests and diseases will increase crop failure and livestock losses. These elements will also disrupt the region's biodiversity, ecosystems, and water and land resources. To succeed in agriculture and address the challenges brought about by this change, producers and governments must adapt.

Although the impact of climate change on agriculture remains uncertain, Western Balkan countries must start devising comprehensive adaptation strategies at all levels of government. Countries should integrate these strategies into cross-sectoral national, regional, and local economic development plans to build farmer and government capacity to cope with the uncertainties of climate change. These plans would focus on measures to address vulnerability to climate change. Current weaknesses include unsustainable farming practices, poor public and private agricultural services and research, limited irrigation infrastructure and water use efficiency, and underdeveloped rural credit and insurance markets. By exploiting EU pre-accession guidance and assistance, Western Balkan countries can mitigate climate change damage to their agri-food sectors.

Key Messages

- Climate change will raise temperatures, reduce rainfall, and cause more frequent droughts, floods, and heat waves. For agriculture this means degraded soil, more pests and diseases, and lower yields, bringing changes to current production systems.
- Exact impacts of climate change remain uncertain; thus, adaptation should focus on building farmer and government capacity to manage uncertainty.
- Starting early will pay dividends later. Investing now in adaptation will limit economic losses from reduced and more variable farm income and food security.
- Better public services for agriculture are essential to building farmer capacity to adapt.
- Climate change adaptation should inform agri-food and rural development strategies and support programs, and be integrated in national, regional, and local economic development plans.

Climate Change Projections for the Western Balkans

Based on current global and regional climate projections, the Western Balkans will become warmer and dryer, with more extreme weather (droughts and floods). The IPCC's global climate projections use general circulation models, driven by emission scenarios based on population growth, economic growth, technological advances, and other factors.[2] Each scenario is associated with a different level of global carbon dioxide emissions and thus has a different effect on projected temperature increases. The EU has produced regional climate models for Europe.[3] What do these models tell us about climate change in the Western Balkans?

Rising Temperatures

The emission scenarios and climate models project large variations in climate conditions, but all show temperatures increasing substantially. The IPCC's projections of global mean annual temperature increases range from 1.1°C to 6.4°C at the end of the 21st century[4]—and the EU projects increases from 2.7°C to 3.9°C across Europe, with a median case projection of 3.1°C.[5] In the Western Balkans, mean annual temperatures are expected to increase 3.5–4.5°C in the median case scenario, with the highest increases in Albania, fYR Macedonia, the southern parts of Bosnia and Herzegovina, Serbia, and Montenegro (map 5.1). Temperature increases would be higher in summer than in winter.[6]

Less Precipitation

In the median case scenario, annual mean precipitation is expected to fall 5–20 percent along the Adriatic coast and the southeastern tip of the Western Balkans, including Albania and fYR Macedonia, with the greatest decrease during the summer (map 5.2). The region's northwestern tip will see a slight increase in precipitation (around 5 percent).

More Floods, Droughts, and Heat Waves

The Western Balkan countries are also expected to experience more extreme weather. Warmer temperatures and less precipitation will increase the frequency and length of heat waves and droughts. And even in areas with a lower mean precipitation, the intensity of precipitation will increase—bringing a higher risk of floods.[7] Recent extreme weather bears testimony to this trend: the Danube River flooded in Serbia in August 2002, while heat waves engulfed the region in the summers of 2003 and 2007. Economic losses caused by major droughts were estimated at $408 million in Bosnia and Herzegovina in 2003 (where they were most frequent), $25 million Albania in 1989–91, and $10 million in fYR Macedonia in 1993.[8]

How Will Climate Change Affect the Agri-food Sector?

The medium- and long-term impact of climate change on agriculture remains uncertain. For example, though regional climate models for Europe are improving, they are inaccurate when applied to the present, projecting dryer and warmer climate conditions than currently prevail.[9] In addition, agro-economic models (such as crop yield models) do not account for new biotechnologies, long-term agricultural land use patterns, or policy and institutional responses—all of which may mitigate vulnerability to climate change. Higher temperatures, reduced precipitation, and more frequent and intense extreme weather would have a profound impact on agricultural production in the Western Balkans.[10]

Map 5.1. Future Temperature Increases in the Western Balkans

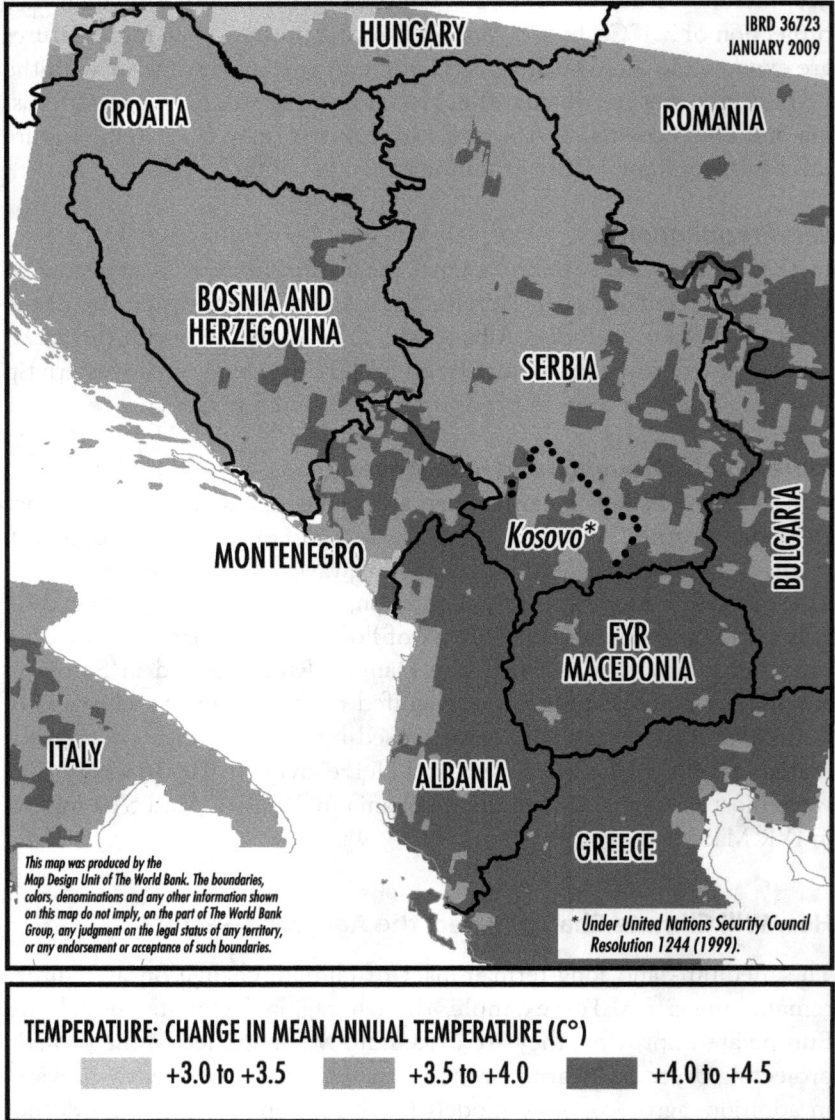

IBRD 36723
JANUARY 2009

HUNGARY

CROATIA

ROMANIA

BOSNIA AND
HERZEGOVINA

SERBIA

BULGARIA

Kosovo*

MONTENEGRO

FYR
MACEDONIA

ITALY

ALBANIA

GREECE

This map was produced by the
Map Design Unit of The World Bank. The boundaries,
colors, denominations and any other information shown
on this map do not imply, on the part of The World Bank
Group, any judgment on the legal status of any territory,
or any endorsement or acceptance of such boundaries.

* Under United Nations Security Council
Resolution 1244 (1999).

TEMPERATURE: CHANGE IN MEAN ANNUAL TEMPERATURE (C°)

+3.0 to +3.5   +3.5 to +4.0   +4.0 to +4.5

Source: Data from European Commission 2007b.

Note: Change in Mean Annual Temperature between 1961–90 and 2071–2100

Map 5.2. Rainfall Will Decline in the Western Balkans

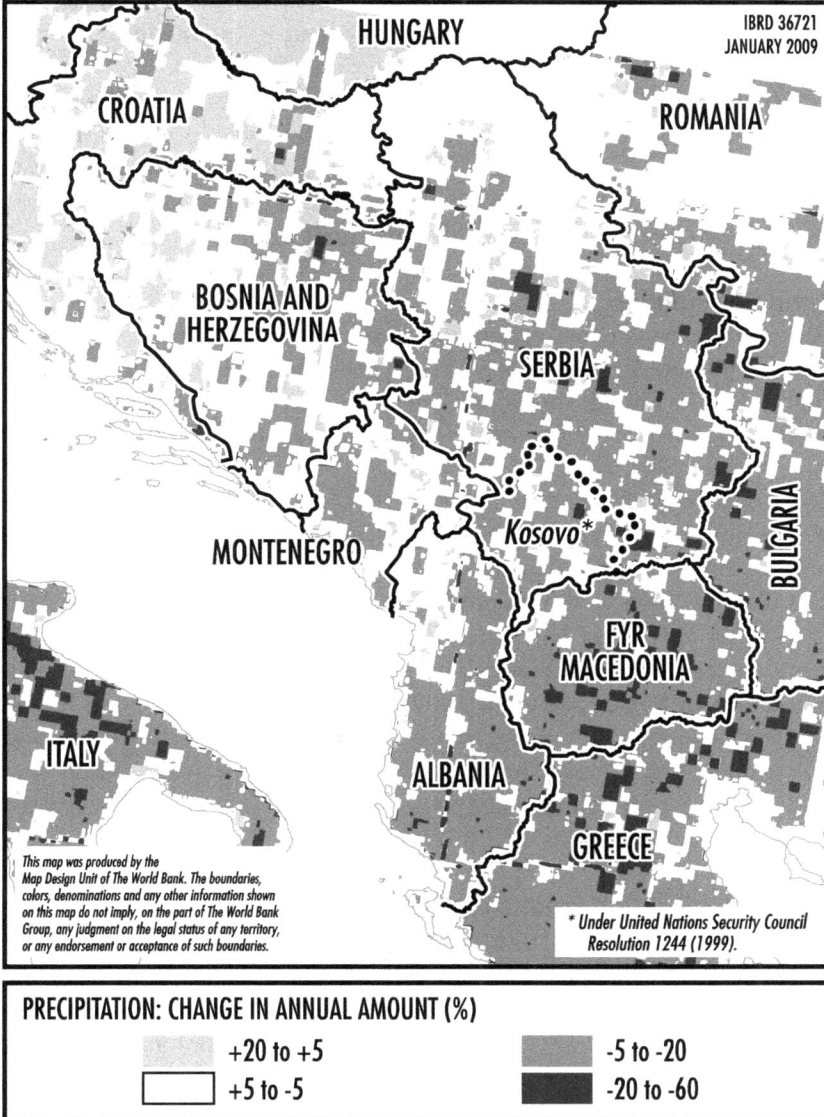

PRECIPITATION: CHANGE IN ANNUAL AMOUNT (%)

+20 to +5

+5 to -5

-5 to -20

-20 to -60

Source: Data from European Commission 2007b.

Note: Change in Mean Annual Precipitation between 1961–90 and 2071–2100

Lower Yields

Except in Bosnia and Herzegovina and northwestern Serbia, the EU expects crop yields to decline up to 10 percent in the median case projection and up to 30 percent in the upper case (map 5.3).

Because plants need carbon dioxide, some studies suggest that certain crop yields might improve with rising carbon dioxide concentrations, through carbon fertilization.[11] But recent field experiments indicate that crop moisture deficits and nitrogen deficiencies could reduce plant responses to higher carbon dioxide concentrations.[12]

Land Degradation

Researchers expect that agricultural production in the Western Balkans will be hindered by land degradation from soil erosion. For example, high-intensity rainfall may cause a loss of organic soil matter as well as more flooding. Droughts may dry topsoil and weaken soil structure.

More Pests and Diseases

The region is expected to see more crop failures and livestock losses from greater exposure to indigenous and nonindigenous vector-borne pests and diseases, such as the bluetongue virus, African horse sickness, African swine fever, West Nile fever, Rift Valley fever, and Crimean-Congo hemorrhagic fever. The bluetongue virus killed an estimated 1.5–2 million sheep in Europe between 1998 and 2005—the longest and largest outbreak on record.[13] Warmer winter temperatures allow for higher pest survival rates, more pest reproduction cycles per growing season, and wider spreads of nonindigenous pest species (which are currently limited by colder temperatures).

Altered Agricultural Production Systems

Climate change will affect various agriculture production systems in the Western Balkans differently (table 5.1). Vegetable production systems, for instance, will become more dependent on irrigation and greenhouses to cope with reduced summer precipitation and greater heat stress. Meanwhile, fruit production systems in rainfed agricultural areas may need to adopt more drought-resilient species (olives, figs, and citrus trees). Although many vineyards are irrigated and thus less vulnerable to changes in precipitation, plant pests and diseases will require more integrated pest management. And as fodder from pastures declines, livestock production systems will need more supplemental feed (table 5.2).

Map 5.3. Much of the Western Balkans Will See Declining Yields

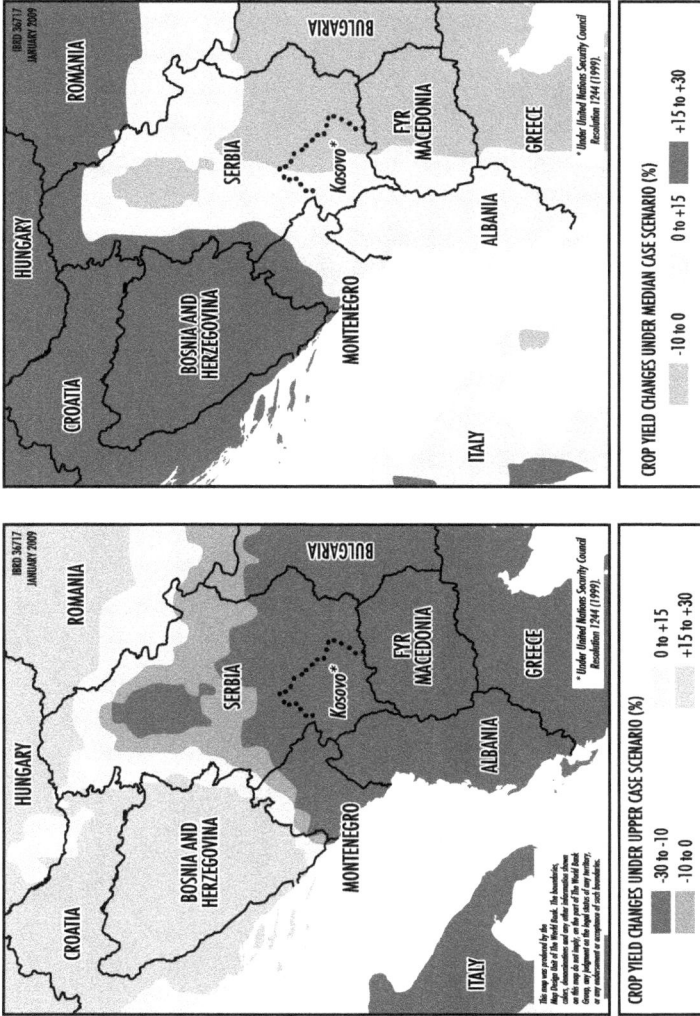

CROP YIELD CHANGES UNDER UPPER CASE SCENARIO (%)

-30 to -10

-10 to 0

0 to +15

+15 to +30

* Under United Nations Security Council Resolution 1244 (1999).

CROP YIELD CHANGES UNDER MEDIAN CASE SCENARIO (%)

-10 to 0

0 to +15

+15 to +30

* Under United Nations Security Council Resolution 1244 (1999).

Source: Data from European Commission 2007b.

Note: Change in Mean Annual Crop Yield between 1961–90 and 2071–2100

Table 5.1. Climate Change Impact on Vegetable, Fruit, and Field Crop Production Systems in the Western Balkans

Agricultural production system	Irrigated		Rainfed	
	Short term	Medium to long term	Short term	Medium to long term
Horticulture Solanacae (tomatoes, peppers, potatoes) Cucurbitacae (cucumbers, zuchinis) Spinacea (spinach) Beets (chards) Leguminous (beans, peas) Allium (onions, garlic) Brassica oleracea (cabbage, broccoli)	Grown throughout the Western Balkans for regional consumption but increasingly also for Western European markets, these crops are often planted in greenhouses and transplanted to fields in March for harvest in June. Most of these crops are in two rotations, with solanacae or leguminous in summer and fall and the more hardy and fast-growing varieties in spring.	Planting of these crops will likely increase on small and intensive farms in most Western Balkan countries. But demand for water due to higher temperatures will increase, and summer horticultural crops without irrigation will become impossible. Cabbages, onions, and leafy vegetables will become an early spring crop, and greenhouses will have to reduce evapotranspiration and prevent sunburn of crops. Mild winters and need for irrigation will require better pest management, including insects, but also mold and various blights, which thrive under greenhouse conditions.	Onions, cabbages, beans, and maize are found on rainfed land in some areas. With warmer temperatures and reduced rainfall, such farming will become riskier, and farmers will have to replace these crops with hardier fodder crops, such as alfalfa, clover, and grains.	With increased heat and less summer rain, rainfed commercial horticulture will likely become unsustainable.

Agricultural production system	Irrigated		Rainfed	
	Short term	Medium to long term	Short term	Medium to long term
Arboriculture Maloideae (apples, pears, quince) Stone fruits (plums, peach apricot, cherries)	Most commercial orchards in the region receive supplemental irrigation at fruit formation. They are generally relatively intensively held.	This pattern of orchards will likely remain. More heat-resistant varieties will likely be adopted, especially for apples and cherries. With milder winters, more pests will require better integrated pest management.	Most household orchards are not irrigated and have varying yields from year to year. Some areas already grow a few citrus fruit and fig trees. Except in southern Albania and Montenegro, olives are rarely found in the region.	More drought-resilient species and late-maturing crops will likely be adopted. Olives, figs, and citrus trees—widely present in Albania and Montenegro—could become common in the rest of the Western Balkans.
Viniculture Zilavka, Vranac, and Blatina	Many vineyards in the Western Balkans receive supplemental irrigation at the time of grape formation. This is common for table grapes as well as wine-making grapes.	Grape farming will become more dependent on irrigation, but wine production volumes will not be affected signifcantly. Disease will likely grow as winters become milder, requiring more integrated pest management year round.	Small household vineyards are largely rainfed, though often supplemented at grape formation with household water.	Water demand by vineyards will increase due to higher evapotranspiration—without supplemental water, grape farming might become impossible in some areas.
Field crops Potato Wheat Oilseeds (sunflower, rapeseed, canola) Peanuts Soya bean Corn and maize	The main irrigated field crops are maize and potatoes, but some peanuts, oil seeds, and soybeans are currently grown.	With higher demand and increasing cost for water, irrigated fields will be sown with higher-value crops, including new crops rarely found in the region, such as soybeans, peanuts, and various oilseeds that thrive under warm climates.	Rainfed crops are typically wheat and other grain crops as well as fodder. Due to the small holdings, production of fodder is largely inadequate with livestock left grazing on land that cannot be cultivated.	Rainfed crops will become riskier, especially grain crops. Cultivation on hillsides will become more precarious, and maintaining constant vegetative cover will become more important to contain erosion.

(continues on next page)

Table 5.1. Climate Change Impact on Vegetable, Fruit, and Field Crop Production Systems in the Western Balkans (continued)

Agricultural production system	Irrigated		Rainfed	
	Short term	Medium to long term	Short term	Medium to long term
Fodder Grass Alfalfa Barley Oats Clover	The main irrigated fodder currently produced is alfalfa. Wheat can be seen in some places. Corn is produced mostly for human consumption. There is very little silage production, especially in the southwestern part of the Western Balkans.	As conditions become drier, irrigated fodder will become important for supporting commercial production of cattle and small ruminants. To maximize irrigated lands, winter grains and clover could be harvested in silage and fields rotated to a higher-value crop for the summer.	Pasture is the largest area dedicated to fodder in the Western Balkans. Pastures are largely unmanaged, with very little fertilization, seeding, or grazing rotations. While some areas are overgrazed, others are underused.	Pasture management will become increasingly important to maintain the vegetative cover of mountain ranges and hillsides. More drought in the summer and heavier rains in the winter are likely to generate higher erosion and soil loss. Increased fodder production in irrigated areas will be necessary to compensate the shortfalls of pastures.

Source: Authors' compilation based on Cline 2007; World Bank 2005; World Bank 2008b; World Bank 2008i; Steinfeld and Mäki-Hokkonen 1995; Kellems 2002; Critchley and Siegert 1991.

Table 5.2. Climate Change Impact on Livestock Production Systems in the Western Balkans

Livestock production system	Short-term	Medium- to long-term
Poultry	Large-scale commercial poultry production in the Western Balkans is relatively uncommon. Most poultry is still free-range household poultry, fed mostly with food scraps and produce from the farm. This is recognized as a key factor in the region's high risk of avian flu and other zoonoses.	Although not necessarily driven by climate change, production will increasingly be concentrated indoors, where feeding habits, inspections, and zoonotic conditions can be better controlled.
Pigs	Pork production methods vary across the Western Balkans. While Serbia has significant commercial installations, pork production in the rest of the region is mostly at household farms and fed from farm produce and scraps. As with poultry, dispersed ownership increases the risk of zoonoses.	As with poultry, pork production is likely to become more concentrated to remain profitable. Consolidation will also be partially driven by requirements of inspection and zoonotic control. The likelihood of disease, such as African swine pest (currently observed in Azerbaijan), to become prevalent is significant.
Sheep and goats	Sheep and goats are held mostly in pastoral. While organized communal grazing is available, many small ruminants, especially in households, are left grazing around the house without much supervision. Animals are not managed intensively, and thus reproduction and growth rates are relatively low.	The longer dry season will require more intensive management of small ruminants, with increased supplemental feeding in the later part of the summer. Supplemental feed would most likely come from silage or hay harvested from rainfed areas in the spring or from winter crops harvested from irrigated areas.
Dairy cows and beef cattle	Dairy cows and beef cattle are held in small numbers by many rural households, largely for household consumption. Large numbers of dairy cows are held to the natural calving cycles in spring, and seasonal milk production varies greatly. Beef cattle are similarly held on marginal land around the farm, with poor grazing rotations and much wasted fodder early in the year and insufficient fodder in the later parts of summer.	As with other animals, dairy cows and beef cattle will be increasingly held in a more concentrated manner for economic and management reasons. The increased concentration will also allow for the production of more manure and slurry, which will be increasingly important to manage organic matter and soil fertility of rainfed lands. The importance of adequate grazing rotations, early hay-making, or silage production, with proper rations of supplemental feed, will increase as the fodder from pastures reduces. Closer care and management to improve cattle productivity will be necessary for the commercial livestock holder.

Source: Authors' compilation based on Cline 2007; World Bank 2005; World Bank 2008b; Steinfeld and Mäki-Hokkonen 1995; Kellems 2002; Critchley and Siegert 1991.

Adapting to Climate Change

Even if global action on climate change substantially reduces greenhouse gas emissions, the impacts of climate change will likely only intensify during this century. Facing various constraints—limited irrigation infrastructure, small land size, low productivity, high input costs, weak rural infrastructure, and underdeveloped rural credit markets—the Western Balkans agri-food sector appears less resilient to climatic change than other regions of Europe. Limited investment in research and development, animal and plant health control, and extension services further constrains agriculture's resilience. Unless investment in adaptation increases, reduced and more variable farm income and food security will likely magnify economic losses.

As a first step, Western Balkan countries should start developing—in close cooperation with all relevant stakeholders—comprehensive adaptation strategies for the agri-food sector at all levels of government. These strategies would include a careful evaluation of local risks, vulnerabilities, and adaptation measures. They would have to be integrated in agriculture and rural development support programs and cross-sectoral national, regional, and local economic development plans. Considering that the impact of climate change will not be unidirectional (for example, areas becoming warmer and dryer may still experience extreme precipitation and floods), adaptation strategies should be designed primarily to build farmer and government capacity to manage a range of climate risks.[14]

Adapting Farming Practices

Farmers can implement low-cost, low-risk adaptations to protect themselves from climate change: planting different crop varieties, substituting or relocating crops, changing planting dates, diversifying crops grown, and altering farming practices to reduce soil erosion. Soil management measures to maintain soil organic carbon—such as decreasing tillage intensity or no tillage practices—sustain soil quality by preventing erosion, and also reduce greenhouse gas emissions and contribute to sequestering carbon dioxide from the atmosphere. And by using fertilizers and pesticides more efficiently, farmers can maintain water quality by protecting supplies from excessive nitrate inflow. Technology investments needed to improve agricultural productivity will overall help address climate change technology demands as well.[15]

To help farmers introduce these new practices and technologies, governments would need to broaden the scope of extension services and research programs. Existing knowledge on best-practice approaches can be leveraged for crop variety selection and diversification, among other topics.[16] Governments would need to promote research and innovation in crop and livestock production technologies while ensuring knowledge and technology transfer to farmers. Close collaboration between university and agri-food stakeholders would be critical to ensure that research is tailored to sectoral and farmer needs and that farmers adopt new technologies (see chapter 7).

The governments of the Western Balkans should also start aligning their national agricultural research programs with the structure and priorities areas set out in EU Research Framework Programs and seize upon the opportunities to actively participate in current and future collaborative research projects. The impact of climate change on agricultural production systems increasingly guides EU agriculture research and innovation programs. The EU Seventh Research Framework Program (2007–13) allocated €1.9 billion for research on food, agriculture, and biotechnology. Science, university, agri-food, and other stakeholders in the EU as well as other countries are collaborating on research projects within this framework program. In its 2007/08 work program the EU launched several collaborative research projects on climate change (table 5.3).

Improving Veterinary and Phytosanitary Capacities

Governments can build capacity in animal and plant health control to mitigate the risk of exposure to indigenous and nonindigenous vectorborne pests and diseases. Efficiency of veterinary and phytosanitary inspection services can be boosted with more risk-based inspections. This requires aligning the legislative and regulatory framework on inspections with EU requirements and increasing staffing for directorates and inspectorates (see chapter 4). It also requires investing in information systems, animal identification and registration systems, specialized training in disease awareness, risk assessment, and contingency planning, as well as upgrading reference laboratories for key animal diseases and plant pests.

Strengthening Meteorological Prediction Capacities and Services

Governments can modernize national meteorological services in support of the agri-food sector. For example, remote satellite sensing can monitor water use, soil moisture, and crop production without agrohydrological ground data.[17] Seasonal weather forecasts remain in development, but more accurate routine forecasts (say, over one to seven days) would assist

Table 5.3. Examples of Climate Change–related EU Research under the 2007/08 Work Program

Project	Description
Annual food crops with improved tolerance to multiple abiotic stresses	This project will support climate-proof food crops that better use agricultural areas affected by erratic rainfall, drought, and other stress in the Mediterranean region. The long-term aim is to stabilize yield capacity in cultivars adapted to combinations of abiotic stresses. The work will integrate research on agricultural systems and husbandry practices (including biofertilizers and plant breeding). It will also address socioeconomic aspects to ensure field applicability and sustainability in different pedoclimatic conditions encountered around the Mediterranean.
Improving animal health and product quality and performance of organic and low-input livestock systems through integration of breeding and innovative management techniques	Different breeding concepts will be analyzed for achieving specific breeding aims (health condition, tolerance to stress, product quality) for organic and low-input rearing of livestock. To produce high-quality and differentiated food products, farm-level indicators will be developed and tested in different breeding programs, integrating management and feeding practices in different macroclimatic regions. The project should reduce the gap between the genetic potential of livestock and their sites and environments. The work may address production systems for cattle, pig, small ruminant, and poultry, also desirable for tourism, rural development, and landscape management. For organic and low-input livestock production, regionally adapted breeding strategies will be compatible with sustainable production, high product quality, and organic principles.
Emerging vectorborne diseases—especially West Nile fever, Rift Valley fever, and Crimean-Congo hemorrhagic fever	West Nile fever, Rift Valley fever, and Crimean-Congo hemorrhagic fever, all arthropod-borne diseases in domestic and wild animals, can also affect humans. West Nile fever outbreaks have already occurred in Europe, and Rift Valley fever and Crimean-Congo hemorrhagic fever are in neighboring countries. This project will create in the EU a network of laboratories and scientists with expertise in these diseases, contributing to the community animal health policy and improving the EU's response to outbreaks of disease.

Source: European Commission 2008.

in timing fertilizing and pest and disease control, enable timely sowing, plowing, irrigation, and harvesting, and limit frost damage. Timely and accurate forecasting that supports better emergency warning systems and preparation, flood zoning and insurance, and water management under drought circumstances might mitigate the economic losses caused by extreme weather. By sharing data, the countries of the Western Balkans could reduce the required investments.

Improving Water Use and Management

Farmers can also optimize irrigation techniques and systems. Governments could increase investments in the rehabilitation and construction of efficient irrigation and drainage schemes and promote rainwater recycling systems and water-saving technologies, such as drip irrigation, to improve water access and availability. Remote satellite sensing data could enforce cost recovery of public investment. Governments can also increase the sustainability of these systems and improve water use efficiency by appropriately pricing water to recover the costs of coping with climate change and by promoting public awareness. Governments would have to ensure sound water management—nationally and regionally—to address scarcity and competing demands.

Managing Risk through Index-based Crop and Livestock Insurance

Governments can foster index-based crop and livestock insurance markets and develop rural credit markets to mitigate climate shocks. Both actions would be mutually reinforcing: agricultural insurance would lower the cost of borrowing while increasing borrower willingness to bear the risk of collateralized loans. Access to credit would reduce farmer vulnerability to climate change by supporting investment in new technologies, limiting distress sales, and diversifying income sources. Index-based insurance, in turn, would mitigate the impact of climate shocks on farm incomes and government budgets. It would also reduce risk associated with adopting more sustainable agricultural technologies, especially for land management.

Index-based insurance is not widely used in the EU because of subsidized crop insurance based on individual loss adjustments.[18] Such crop insurance schemes have often proven to be fiscally expensive, to cover only the large, commercial farms, and have failed to eliminate the need for disaster assistance. Several approaches are being explored to adapt index-based insurance to diverse conditions (box 5.1), but because all are still in pilot stages, no definitive conclusions can be drawn.[19] The indicator of choice depends on the coverage and availability of historical data on climate, crop yields, and livestock mortality. A high correlation between the indicator and farmer losses would lower the basis risk.

Index-based insurance has many advantages. Objectively measured, it is the same for all farmers. It minimizes adverse selection, avoids drawing up and monitoring individual contracts, and reduces administrative costs. This would make insurance affordable to more farmers. Index-based insurance would also be reinsurable in international markets, diversifying

Box 5.1

Index-based Livestock Insurance in Mongolia

Since 2005 Mongolia has piloted index-based livestock insurance to share risks among herders, insurance companies, and the government. The project combines self-insurance, market-based insurance, and social insurance. Herders retain small losses that do not affect the viability of their business (self-insurance), while larger losses are transferred to the private insurance industry (market insurance through a base insurance product). The government bears the final layer of catastrophic losses (social insurance through a disaster-response product).

Herders pay a market premium rate for the base insurance product, which pays out to individual herders when the livestock mortality rate in a local region exceeds a certain threshold. Because excess mortality reflects dry, windy summers and cold, high-snowfall winters, the insurance index is linked not to a weather event but to historical data on livestock mortality. Insurance payments are thus based on local mortality rather than an individual's livestock losses, reducing moral hazards, adverse selection, and costs.

The key is having good data to develop the livestock mortality index and determining specific mortality rates that trigger indemnity payments. Mongolia has a 33-year time series on adult animal mortality for all regions and for the four major species (cattle and yak, horse, sheep, and goat).

Source: World Bank 2005.

a country's weather risk across geographical areas. Governments in the Western Balkans could foster index-based insurance by establishing a favorable legal and regulatory framework, facilitating collaborative arrangements with other countries in the region to create a critical mass of subscribers, improving information sources, and raising awareness among farmers of different insurance opportunities.

Integration with Public Strategies and Support Programs

Identifying adequate short- and medium-term adaptation measures and a program for their implementation is central to any adaptation strategy for the agri-food sector. To ensure policy coherence and enhance the effect, adaptation measures should effectively inform agri-food and rural development strategies and support programs and should be integrated in cross-sectoral national, regional, and local economic development plans. Adequate monitoring and evaluation to assess the impact of the measures would be critical to help inform and guide future decision-making on climate change risk management.

Governments in the Western Balkans should use EU agriculture and rural development policies as a reference in building their adaptive capacity and take advantage of EU pre-accession assistance for rural development. Sustainable development of agri-food is now prominent in the CAP and the EU IPARD program. In addition to requiring compliance with environmental and animal and plant health standards, the program cofinances farm investments, environmental protection in rural areas, and diversification of rural economic activities for potential beneficiaries among farmers and processors. All these measures help reduce farmers' sensitivity to climate change. The countries of the Western Balkans should leverage this assistance to help alleviate the various climate change constraints facing their farmers.

Notes

1. IPCC 2007a.
2. These models comprise four scenario families. A1 includes very rapid economic growth, global population that peaks mid-century then declines, and rapid introduction of more efficient technologies. Carbon dioxide emissions will depend on three scenarios for energy technologies: fossil fuel–intensive, balanced, and predominantly non–fossil fuel. A2 includes high population growth. Economic growth and technological change are fragmented and slow, while emissions are high. B1 includes rapid changes to a service and information economy, reductions in material intensity, clean and efficient technologies, and relatively low emissions. B2 includes intermediate economic development but less rapid and more diverse technological change, resulting in slightly higher emissions than B1. These scenario families are laid out in the *Special Report on Emission Scenarios*, prepared by the IPCC for the *Third Assessment Report* in 2001. It replaced the scenarios used for the *Second Assessment Report* in 1995. The *Special Report on Emission Scenarios* was also used in the panels' *Fourth Assessment Report* in 2007.
3. The EU attempted to improve the reliability of projections for Europe by downscaling general circulation models to produce models that can be applied to spatial scales of 50 or even 20 kilometers (see Quiroga and Iglesias 2007). See http://prudence.dmi.dk/ for more information on the EU–funded Prediction of Regional Scenarios and Uncertainties for Defining European

Climate Change Risks and Effects research project, which was implemented under the Fifth Framework Program for Energy, Environment, and Sustainable Development (1999–2002).

4. For 2090–99 relative to 1980–99 (IPCC 2007b).

5. For 2071–2100 relative to 1061–1990. These projections are for the SERS A2 and B2 scenario families (Quiroga and Iglesias 2007)

6. IPCC 2007a.

7. IPCC 2007a.

8. World Bank 2007a.

9. World Bank 2008e.

10. See the EU's Project of Economic Impacts of Climate Change in Sectors of the European Union Based on Bottom-up Analysis research project for more information (http://peseta.jrc.es/).

11. Cline 2007.

12. Cline 2007.

13. Baylis and Githeko 2006.

14. World Bank forthcoming.

15. Binswanger-Mkhize 2008.

16. World Bank forthcoming.

17. World Bank 2008b.

18. Bielza and others 2007.

19. World Bank 2007e.

PART III

Making Rural Areas Competitive

To shift to a competitive agri-food sector as described in chapter 2 and to be ready for the challenges described in part II, governments in the Western Balkans need appropriate frameworks for assistance and incentives. One key aspect of future public policies will be a clearer distinction between agricultural policies that support commercial entities competing in the market, broader rural development policies that foster alternative income sources in rural areas, and better social protection policies that ensure minimum living conditions for the poor.

Practical long-term goals for the agri-food sector in the Western Balkans are to increase efficiency and competitiveness and to take advantage of opportunities in high-value markets. This has already started in response to intense competition from regional markets. Success will depend on spreading knowledge for higher productivity and technical efficiency, on making major capital investments in farms and in processing facilities, on retraining human capital (technical, marketing, financial), on updating legal, institutional, and fiscal frameworks, and on using modern marketing techniques.

The private sector will finance part of these efforts, but some critical areas require judicious public funding to catalyze and leverage private investment. Otherwise, a modern agri-food sector in the Western Balkans will be much more slow to develop and more likely to lose ground to neighboring countries. Areas requiring particular attention from public authorities include agricultural information systems, agricultural education and extension services, and competitive grants for upgrading farm and processing facilities to meet higher food quality and safety standards.

A key challenge is to include commercially oriented producers in the modernizing agri-food sector. Competition among downstream players should help, but not all producers will adapt to more fluid consumer-driven food chains. Governments will be tempted to continue supporting nonviable farm structures for social and political reasons. But to make agriculture more productive and competitive, the sector needs to shed labor—and assisting these displaced workers is a key to a healthy rural sector.

Part II identified challenges facing the agri-food and rural sector in the Western Balkans as well as specific actions to deal with the challenges. Part III looks more broadly at what governments need to do: chapter 6 looks at the overall strategy and structure of public expenditures, and chapter 7 at how money is spent on public agricultural services.

CHAPTER 6

Strategies to Modernize

The promise of joining the EU has increased government resources for the agri-food sector in the Western Balkans—as governments ramp up spending to fulfill institutional requirements and as EU pre-accession funds start to flow. This chapter explores how to use these new resources to modernize the sector and transform rural space. With the right policy framework and incentives, governments in the Western Balkans can foster a competitive agri-food sector. But they must consider the dual function of agriculture in the region: as a contributor to economic growth—reducing agri-food trade deficits—and as a social buffer—mitigating rural unemployment and poverty. While agricultural policies need to develop a competitive agri-food sector, rural development policies need to spur diversified and knowledge-based economic growth in rural areas and to reduce dependency on semisubsistence agriculture as a poverty alleviation measure.

Public spending on agriculture can increase agricultural GDP. Contributing most strongly to this growth is investment in rural infrastructure (primarily irrigation and roads) and in research and development.[1] However, spending increases will not be effective in supporting a modern agri-food sector if the focus of current allocations remain the same as now—that is, for ad hoc production-linked subsidies at the expense of rural development programs. The wrong support (subsidies linked to production, prices, or specific crops) risks trapping many people in low-level agriculture and perpetuating large public support programs—rather than creating a vibrant agri-food sector and rural space.

Key Messages

- Sector support as a share of government spending will continue to increase because of the EU pre-accession process. But the type and amount of support most governments in the Western Balkans currently provide will not foster modernization.
- More and better rural development policies and measures that promote investment in competitiveness are needed. Alignment with the CAP in its future form will ease this transition.
- Building EU–compliant institutions in a timely and planned manner can help modernize the agri-food sector.

A Framework for Effective Agricultural Public Expenditures

Support for modernization includes investment support through rural development programs and the delivery of agricultural services. The EU model of agricultural support is moving toward such measures that stimulate more efficient investment in agriculture as opposed to direct production and market support. Future EU policies thus provide a more effective and nondistortionary model of agricultural support for countries to emulate, now and later, to meet EU accession requirements.

Governments in the Western Balkans are already increasing agricultural spending and will continue to do so as they access EU pre-accession assistance. They are also aligning their agricultural policies with EU policies to avoid shocks at accession. This is wise and necessary given the importance and complexity of EU agricultural policy. But policymakers must anticipate profound ongoing changes in the CAP, whose aim has been shifting from boosting agricultural production to reducing surplus production, as well as encouraging environmentally sustainable farming and income diversification. Thus, aligning with current EU policies not only risks creating bad policy but also wasted effort. This section looks in depth at this future agricultural support model of the EU and discusses why alignment with this model will be critical for the Western Balkan countries.

More Funds Will Become Available for Agricultural Development
Overall public spending on agriculture in the Western Balkans remains lower than in other regions, even when adjusted to the size of the agri-food sector (table 6.1). In the Western Balkans public expenditure on agriculture accounts for 0.02–0.08 percent of GDP (adjusted to the size

Table 6.1. Agriculture Expenditures Are Generally Low: International Comparison of Fiscal Transfers to Agriculture, 2002–07 (percent)

Country	Agriculture as share of GDP	Agricultural spending as share of total GDP	Ratio of agriculture as a share of GDP to agricultural spending as share of GDP (adjusted to size of the agri-food sector)
Western Balkans			
Albania	23	0.50	0.02
Bosnia and Herzegovina	11	0.70	0.06
Macedonia, fYR	12	0.60	0.05
Montenegro	10	0.70	0.07
Serbia	13	0.92	0.08
OECD			
European Union	2.3	0.65	0.28
United States	1.6	0.73	0.46
Australia	3.0	0.31	0.10
Canada	2.3	0.51	0.22

Source: World Bank 2007e.

of the agri-food sector), compared with 0.10–0.46 percent for OECD countries. Spending intensity in terms of spending per farm unit, hectare of land, or rural population is highest in Montenegro and Serbia and lowest in Albania and Bosnia and Herzegovina. Agricultural support, in terms of the share of fiscal transfers in agricultural GDP, is highest in Montenegro and Serbia and lowest in Albania and fYR Macedonia. Higher spending can boost sector competitiveness and prepare countries for EU candidacy (or for member status, in the case of fYR Macedonia), covering costs of institutions needed for accession and for accessing EU pre-accession assistance. In recent years spending on agriculture and the rural sector has risen significantly in all Western Balkan countries except for Albania—reflecting the importance that governments are attaching to the agri-food sector for economic development and further EU integration (figure 6.1).[2]

Funds will continue to increase as countries receive EU pre-accession assistance. To help candidate and potential candidate countries meet EU standards during pre-accession, and to assist with rural and regional development, the EU distributes pre-accession assistance through

Figure 6.1. Agricultural Expenditures Are Increasing as a Share of Overall Government Expenditures: Change in Agricultural and Central Government Spending

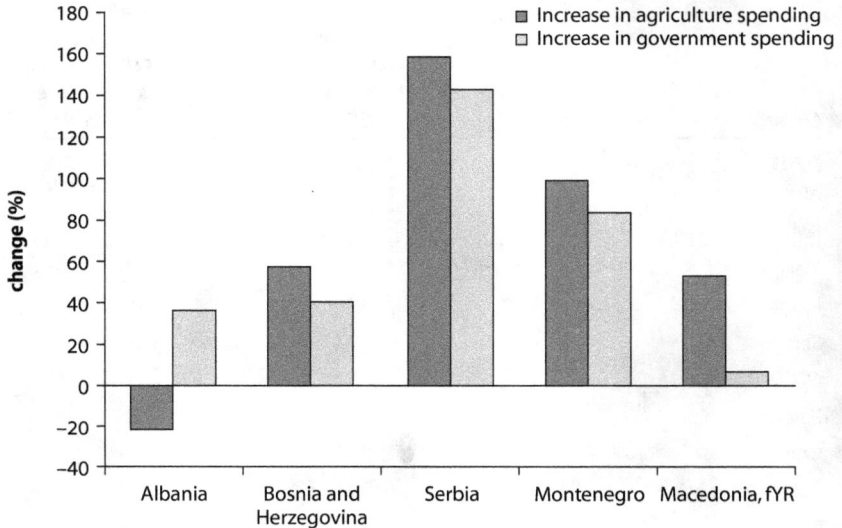

Note: Data for Albania are for 2002-06. Data for Bosnia and Herzegovina are for 2002-06. Data for Data for Serbia are for 2001-05. Data for Montenegro are for 2002–07. Data for fYR Macedonia are for 2001-05.

Source: Ministries of Agriculture and Ministries of Finance of Albania, Bosnia and Herzegovina, fYR Macedonia, Montenegro, and Serbia.

the IPA, including rural development funds through the EU IPARD program. Pre-accession assistance funds in the order of 1.0–4.4 percent of their 2006 GDP a year are projected to be available to the Western Balkan countries under the IPA program (table 6.2), a substantial increase in public expenditure.[3] And they are likely to access 20–30 percent of their 2006 agricultural spending under the EU IPARD program (see table 6.2).

Aligning Public Policies with the Future CAP Is Critical

This section looks at the evolution of the CAP since its inception and discusses how agricultural policies can be aligned with it.

The CAP: A Moving Target. The CAP was created in 1960 to provide subsidies and guaranteed prices for farmers to increase production. In the 1970s and 1980s the EU reached self-sufficiency for most agricultural products and has since had almost permanent surpluses of major farm commodities—whose subsidized export and disposal have distorted world

Table 6.2. Potential Pre-Accession Assistance and Estimated Amounts and Costs of IPARD Funding, 2007–11

Country	Pre-accession assistance (€ millions)						Average annual IPA funds 2007–11 (% of 2006 GDP)[a]	Projected annual IPARD allocation (€ millions)	IPARD allocation		Cost of IPARD as share of agricultural spending (%)	Total IPARD operating costs (€ millions)
	2007	2008	2009	2010	2011	Average, 2007–11			Share of agricultural spending (%)	Share of GDP (%)		
Albania	61	71	81	93	95	80.2	1.1	10	21	0.13	8	4
Bosnia and Herzegovina	62	75	89	106	108	88.0	1.0	23	23	0.23	9	9
Macedonia, fYR	58	70	82	92	99	80.2	4.4	9	31	0.19	12	3
Montenegro	31	33	33	34	35	33.2	1.8	5	27	0.23	10	2
Serbia	190	191	195	199	203	195.6	1.1	46	22	0.26	9	18

Source: Authors' calculations based on data from European Commission 2007c and World Bank 2006a, 2006b, 2007d.

a. An estimated 21 percent of combined non-IPARD EU financial assistance is assumed for all countries except fYR Macedonia, for which the average annual IPARD allocation from the Multi-Annual Indicative Financial Framework is shown. This framework foresees an average annual IPARD allocation for fYR Macedonia of €9.1 million from 2007 to 2011, representing 31 percent of its 2006 agricultural spending. The estimates for other countries, which are all potential EU candidate countries, assume that they receive IPARD funds for approximately 21 percent of their combined non-IPARD EU financial assistance. This projection is based on the experience of the new member states, where average SAPARD allocations from 2000 to 2004 were 11–31 percent, or on average 21 percent, of combined PHARE allocations.

markets. The annual cost of the CAP rose rapidly, passing €40 billion in 1997. It comprised about 60 percent of the total EU budget in 1989 and 40 percent in 2007. It is estimated to fall to around 35 percent by 2013.

The last 25 years have seen continual attempts to reform the CAP. The 1992 MacSharry reforms were intended to limit rising cost increases and were accompanied by efforts to adapt the CAP to a more liberal agricultural market. The reforms reduced support (for example, by 29 percent for cereals), set aside funds to withdraw land from production, and encouraged retirement, forestation, and environmentally friendly farming. In 2003 more significant reforms were introduced because of rising costs, WTO demands for trade liberalization, increased attention to the environment, and a drop in agriculture's political and economic importance. Strict budgetary ceilings and financing limits for Pillar 1 of the CAP, which covers production and market support, were introduced for 2007–13.[4] The CAP now encourages farmers to comply with environmental standards and invest where they have a comparative advantage.

In November 2008, EU agriculture ministers reached a political agreement on proposals developed by the European Commission for the "health check" of the CAP.[5] The objectives of the health check were to simplify direct aid and boost its effectiveness and efficiency, make market support instruments relevant for an expanded EU in a different global environment, and confront such new challenges as climate change, biofuel, water management, and biodiversity protection. Elaborating on the 2003 reforms, the agreement envisages eliminating most of the remaining production-linked payments, increasing the transfer of resources from direct production (Pillar 1) to rural development (Pillar 2), and using market support (public buying of surplus production) only as a safety net (unlikely to be needed with today's high food prices). In addition, set-asides will be abolished, and milk quotas will expire in 2015.

The reformed CAP makes a key distinction between Pillar 1 (traditional market support measures and direct aid to farmers) and Pillar 2 (rural development programs) to reflect the paradigm shift from exclusive agricultural policies to a broader rural development agenda.[6] There has been a gradual trend toward increasing Pillar 2 support, currently 15 percent of the CAP budget. Following the "health check" of the CAP in 2008, funding for rural development under Pillar 2 will be further boosted by allocating more funds to rural development from direct aid. While Pillar 1 expenditures will continue to absorb the bulk of CAP resources, Pillar 2 expenditures will account for about 25 percent of the CAP budget (some €50 billion) by 2013 (figure 6.2).

Figure 6.2. The Importance of Pillar 2 in the CAP Is Increasing

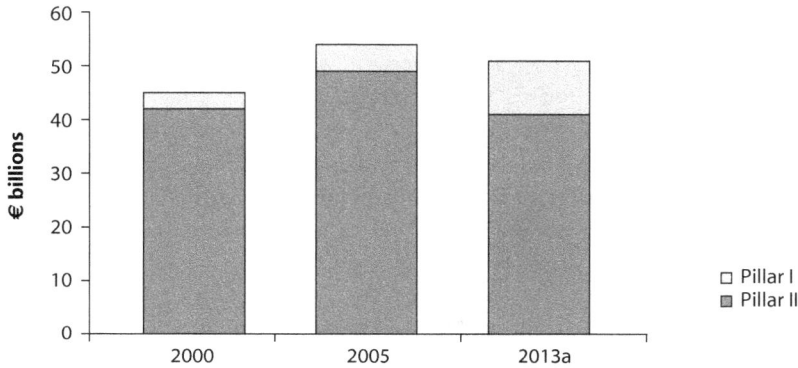

Source: European Commission 2003; European Commission 2005; European Parliament, European Council, and European Commission 2006.
a. Projected.

Main Characteristics of CAP Support. The policy reforms most important for the Western Balkan countries seeking to align with the CAP include decoupling, cross-compliance, and modulation.

Decoupling involves bundling production-linked support into a single farm payment (called the Single Payment Scheme) independent of production. To avoid production abandonment or severe market disturbance, EU member states may maintain some product-specific direct aid under certain conditions.[7]

Cross-compliance was introduced as a precondition to access funds from the Single Payment Scheme to encourage more environmentally friendly farming and better food safety and quality. Direct aid is linked to environmental, food safety, animal and plant health and welfare standards, and good agricultural practices, such as proper use of pesticides and chemical fertilizers.[8] Other criteria include productive land—though this was excluded for 2008 due to high grain prices—and that 2 meters on the perimeter of each field be left for wildlife habitat. With this comes an obligatory farm advisory system to help farmers meet cross-compliance criteria.

Modulation refers to increasing spending for Pillar 2 by reducing Pillar 1 spending. Direct aid to all farms receiving more than €5,000 a year has been reduced by 5 percent, and those funds have been redirected to the rural development budget to finance additional rural development. Following the 2008 CAP health check, this rate will be increased to 10 percent by 2012. Only one percentage point of the modulation money generated in an EU member state will be allocated to that state, and the remaining will be redistributed among EU member states.[9]

Support to agriculture and rural development similar to that under Pillar 2 must be increased—a task already taken on by the Western Balkan countries. According to their strategy documents (see chapter 1), investment in Pillar 2–type support will amount to about 70 percent of combined spending on agriculture and rural development by the end of their implementation period. More rural development support will also prepare countries to absorb EU pre-accession funds under the EU IPARD program when they become available.

Implications for Agriculture and Rural Development Support Programs. The aforementioned reforms contain principles that could guide governments in the Western Balkans to align agricultural policies and support programs with the CAP. These governments should avoid introducing new production-linked support, transform existing production and market support into decoupled single area payments (box 6.1), and emphasize rural development programs over direct aid and market support. Examples from existing EU member states show that rural development policies are more important than agricultural policies in supporting structural changes in rural areas.

In addition, governments in the Western Balkans should encourage cross-compliance and help farmers and processors meet EU and other international standards (see chapter 4). Cross-compliance as a condition for support payments would promote environmental standards and good agricultural practices and would facilitate compliance with the EU

Box 6.1

Romania and Direct Payments: Aligning with the EU

In 2005 Romania, an EU member since January 2007, shifted its agricultural support system to area-based direct payments (limited to the initial 5 hectares per farm). This payment was to be used only to purchase inputs: certified seeds, chemical fertilizers, pesticides, and gas or diesel oil. This support covered nearly two-thirds of the arable area eligible for EU support payments. Agricultural producers who sold on internal markets could benefit from additional product-based subsidies for a range of crops and livestock. Romania focused mainly on supporting the incomes of the small-scale farmers (less than 5 hectares).

emphasis on food safety. Governments should also use administrative elements of the EU IPARD program and the CAP, such as the Paying Agency and the IACS, to control national support policies and measures. These instruments would integrate EU support into overall agricultural support and enhance the transparency of agricultural support policies. And with agricultural information systems, such as a FADN and a market information system, they would improve market transparency and provide for better informed policy planning.

Current Agricultural Support Does Not Promote Modernization

The policy environment for agriculture in the Western Balkans is increasingly taking into account the region's European future. Resources to support the sector are increasing, but policies differ markedly, from limited direct intervention to mechanisms similar to the CAP.

The type of public support to agriculture matters for economic growth and competitiveness. Different policy instruments for public expenditures shape incentives and can help or deter modernization. The biggest problem with production subsidies is that they allow bureaucrats and politicians to "pick the winners"—leading to mistakes, costly market distortions, and wasted money. Government would also be politically responsible for problems in the subsidized sector. Far more effective are instruments and support systems that allow winners to emerge: public goods and services, decoupled payments, and investment support. Studies suggest that investing in public goods—particularly rural infrastructure (irrigation and roads) and better technology—has a greater impact on agricultural growth than do other forms of public spending, including subsidies.[10] In fact, production subsidies, though viewed by some countries as creating a favorable negotiating position when entering the EU, may delay sector modernization because poorly designed instruments encourage noncommercial farmers to remain in the sector regardless of productivity. Instruments that improve productivity will help commercially oriented farmers increase competitiveness, and can be complemented by investments in rural development programs that provide alternatives to smallholders searching for off-farm opportunities.

Production Subsidies Delay Transition

Most countries still provide the bulk of agri-food sector support through Pillar 1-type subsidies (figure 6.3). In recent years some countries have reduced subsidies in favor of agricultural services and rural development,

Figure 6.3. Pillar 1-type Support Tends to Dominate Agricultural Expenditures

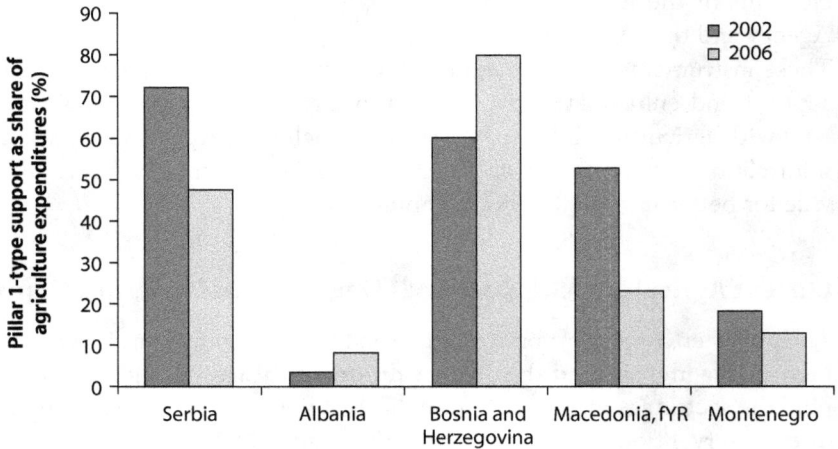

Note Based on national categorization methods for agriculture expenditures.

Source: Authors' calculations based on data from Ministries of Agriculture and Ministries of Finance of Albania, Bosnia and Herzegovina, fYR Macedonia, Montenegro, and Serbia

but further reductions are needed to modernize more quickly. Other countries—such as Bosnia and Herzegovina and (to a lesser extent) Albania—are delaying modernization by increasing subsidies (figure 6.3).[11]

Some countries cite the need to align with the CAP as a reason to increase subsidies; others argue that subsidies improve their negotiating positions for CAP payments. When joining the EU, countries receive CAP funds commensurate with subsidies at the time of accession. But these arguments ignore the CAP's gradual shift away from production-linked support. Spending more on subsidies now may be counterproductive by making it harder to align with the future CAP. In addition, subsidies deter modernization and inflict significant opportunity costs, since money could be spent on more beneficial investment and rural development. Spending more on rural development (Pillar 2) and avoiding increases in direct subsidies and market support (Pillar 1) could move Western Balkan countries more directly toward alignment with future EU agricultural policy. In addition, countries have found it more difficult to spend EU money on direct subsidies and market support and easier to spend it on rural development. And countries that spend more on rural development now are likely to receive more EU money later.

Some Western Balkan countries have direct payment schemes, but others subsidize specific products, such as milk; inputs, such as seeds

(Montenegro), fertilizer (Serbia), and fuel (Albania); and credit (Serbia). Such payments are at best only partially decoupled and still affect production. Most such interventions lack any market failure rationale—and actually distort markets by sending wrong price signals. For milk production, countries emphasize wanting to support disadvantaged (mostly mountainous) areas, but market price support is not the appropriate policy instrument, even though the policy objectives are legitimate. The policies are nontransparent because they are paid for by consumers and not from tax payments, they create market distortions, and they incur a higher fiscal cost than other income transfers do. In addition, a small share of producers may receive the bulk of the public support. The EU has estimated that in 2005 about 57 percent of the transfers in the EU-15 countries went to 6 percent of the producers and about 80 percent of the transfers in the EU-25 countries went to 20 percent of producers.[12]

Insufficient Alignment of Rural Development Support Limits Its Impact

As highlighted in chapter 3, investment in rural development is critical for balanced growth in rural areas. Support to rural development has been increasing (figure 6.4), driven primarily by European integration and preparation of the institutional and legal framework to access EU

Figure 6.4. Pillar 2-type Support Has Increased

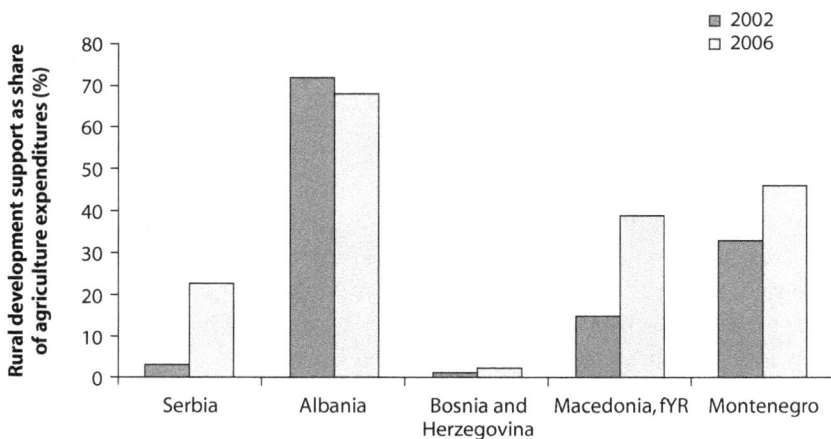

Note: Based on national categorization methods for agriculture expenditures.

Source: Authors' analysis based on data from Ministries of Agriculture and Ministries of Finance of Albania, Bosnia and Herzegovina, fYR Macedonia, Montenegro, and Serbia

pre-accession support.[13] But existing rural development measures are often heavily restricted in access and scope, lack transparent instruments for planning, implementation, and control, and still contain various production subsidy elements.

Countries need to better align their rural development measures with CAP principles. The EU IPARD approach provides a good basis, focusing on agriculture and food processing but also additional and alternative income and employment opportunities for smallholder farmers and rural residents. Serbia's rural development measures are already broadly aligned, supporting investment in farms, measures to improve product quality, investment in rural development, and an early retirement scheme. Montenegro's rural development measures are also on the right track, though some measures not compliant with EU policy remain to be phased out.[14] Albania has yet to adopt a strategy for investing in agriculture and rural development, currently directing 80–90 percent of its investment funds to irrigation and drainage infrastructure and support to agricultural, livestock, and agro-industrial production and marketing. In 2006 fYR Macedonia set up a rural development program and paying agency, and is progressively integrating other forms of agricultural support. This is a step in the right direction, but appropriate rural development support measures still need to be identified.

Governments also need institutional mechanisms to plan and implement rural development measures. Coordination for cross-cutting investments in rural development is often rudimentary. Field-based support services that ensure potential beneficiaries' broad-based access to rural development support are weak. And improved payment and control systems are needed to deliver, monitor, and evaluate rural development measures.

Investments in Agricultural Services Pay Off

Better public agricultural services, such as advisory services (extension) and research and education, are critical for improving competitiveness and preparing the agri-food sector for future challenges (see chapter 7). The benefits can be substantial. In Albania farmers who received extension services—in particular advice on soil quality and soil improvement techniques—were 72 percent more efficient than farmers who did not.[15] Better services will also prepare farmers and the rural population to absorb support for agriculture and rural development under the EU IPARD program. Despite high returns, public expenditure on these systems is often very low: 8–10 percent of public spending on agriculture in fYR Macedonia for 2002–05, among the lowest in the region, and 10–13 percent of the Serbian Ministry of Agriculture, Forestry, and Water Management's budget for 2004–06.[16] While limited allocation for research and advisory services makes sense when much needed institutional reforms are being finalized, increased expenditures will be necessary in the longer term. In addition to spending levels, the quality of these services is critical (addressed in detail in chapter 7).

Management of Public Expenditures

Public spending alone cannot resolve the challenges facing the agri-food and rural sectors in the Western Balkans, but it is critical, so governments need to maximize the impact of their expenditures. In particular, they need to improve planning, implementation, monitoring, and evaluation.

Agricultural and rural development strategies (see chapter 1) define appropriate frameworks for developing the agri-food and rural sector, but institutional shortcomings (inability to predict revenue or to improve weak monitoring and evaluation) hamper implementation of these strategies. Improvement is needed on several fronts to plan agriculture expenditures and manage budgets in the most rational and transparent manner.[17]

Linking Budgets with Policy Objectives

A more strategic approach is needed to link policy objectives with the budget process. Agriculture and rural development strategies have been adopted by all Western Balkan countries, but they are only partially reflected in medium-term expenditure frameworks. Annual agriculture budgets are still based largely on past expenditure patterns and political pressures rather than on priorities described in the strategies.

Governments also need to boost capacity to cost programs and assess their future recurrent cost implications for the budget. Agriculture and rural development strategies estimate only implementation cost (and Serbia's strategy does not provide cost estimates at all), not recurrent costs. Albania has had many strategy documents in recent years, but none of them is closely connected to the budget process or includes clear cost implications of proposed measures or activities.[18]

Government budget execution should also be improved. Some Western Balkan countries experience budget cuts and reallocations during the year, and because of poor cash management, spending can be frozen until cash becomes available again. In Albania the government implements in-year budget cuts and reallocations and has poor procurement processes—undermining the budget as a predictable tool for implementing policy. A review in fYR Macedonia found that budget execution is recorded in accordance with accounting requirements but not followed or analyzed as a management tool by Ministry of Agriculture, Forestry, and Water Management staff.[19]

The allocation of expenditures by functional and economic category should be modified to match the strategic program and to allow for effective planning and monitoring and evaluation. Ideally, agricultural public expenditure should be aligned with agricultural strategy and structured by priority programs, measures, and projects. Expenditure needs to be categorized by economic classification (between personnel, operating expenditures, capital expenditures, subsidies, and transfers) and functional classification (between administration, market and credit support, public agricultural services, and rural development and structural support). In practice, public expenditure allocations often follow the historic budget organization and often apply expenditure categories irrelevant to policy priorities. In Bosnia and Herzegovina the budget classification systems break down expenditures by economic classification only.

Coordinating Cross-Sectoral Activities

Several cross-sectoral actions affecting agriculture and rural development need to be taken outside ministries of agriculture, including encouraging horizontal and vertical integration of value chains through the appropriate legislation, upgrading infrastructure and improving human capital, strengthening the business environment, and promoting land consolidation (see chapters 1–3). Other ministries and government bodies involved in these issues need to be coordinated more effectively. Roads and education—both under different ministries—are crucial to rural development, but the responsibility and coordinating mechanisms among the government bodies with mandates in rural areas remain unclear. Where there are strong subnational entities, as in Bosnia and Herzegovina, harmonized budget planning and execution systems are needed at the entity levels of government, with the state level playing a central coordinating role.[20]

Monitoring and Evaluating Expenditures to Improve Performance

Monitoring and evaluation of public expenditure for agriculture need to improve in all Western Balkan countries. To mobilize additional national and international funds for agriculture and rural development, ministries of agriculture have to demonstrate the efficiency (value for money) and effectiveness (impact) of public spending on investments and services for the sector. While the beneficiaries of services and subsidies are typically known, there is little effort to systematically consolidate spending by purpose (specific measure or type of subsidy) or other useful criteria (type of beneficiary, regional distribution). Throughout the Western Balkans the incomplete farm registers and sector statistics leave little known about the impact of agriculture interventions. Better monitoring and evaluation will also allow the budget to be better executed.

Countries should look to EU best practices, which include a system of expenditure monitoring and evaluation for all EU member states that receive EU funding. The expenditure has to be part of a budget-financed operational program (to avoid off-budget spending). And the most important requirement is suitable, quantifiable objectives (key performance indicators) at different levels (input, output results, impact). The indicators are formulated before the program begins and assessed at completion. The European Commission has issued guidelines for identifying suitable indicators.[21] The U.K. performance-based budget system is an exemplar methodology among EU member states for effectively managing public expenditure.[22]

Institutions and Systems for Administering EU Support Programs

Another important aspect of government support for the agri-food sector involves building the institutions and capacities needed to absorb EU pre-accession assistance under the EU IPARD program and ultimately CAP funds. To demonstrate this capacity, the Western Balkan countries need new institutions, significant modifications to existing institutions, and funds to match EU pre-accession financial assistance. Institutional demands include setting up and staffing a central financial control unit, establishing structures to administer pre-accession funds in accordance with EU accounting and auditing standards, and passing required legislation in a timely manner. Countries have various options for institutional arrangements as long as the system is financially independent.

The cost of these institutions and of administering EU IPARD funds in general will be substantial. In the new EU member states the costs of administering SAPARD funds (the EU's previous pre-accession assistance instrument) were 3–5 percent of the program's funds and national cofinancing requirements combined. Countries also need to cofinance 25 percent of the public aid for EU IPARD projects.[23] Operating funds (for labor and administration of information technology and control systems, for instance) may account for 7–16 percent of agricultural budgets, depending on the number of accredited measures and applications for funding received. There will also be costs to establish and accredit a Paying Agency, create demand for funds, and set up other institutions for EU accession, such as an IACS, including a LPIS, and a FADN. The labor cost of setting up an IACS is estimated at €360,000–720,000 over one year to €1.4 million over two years.[24] Costs for a FADN are estimated at €130,000–220,000.

An IACS, Paying Agency, and FADN will enable the Western Balkan countries to receive the full support for which they will qualify as EU member states. These structures are also an institutional model for sound planning, targeting, administering, and evaluating existing and future support programs in the national budget before accession. Building these institutions is a lengthy process that must be initiated during pre-accession. Starting sooner will mean that institutions can gradually be strengthened and easily become fully functional when needed. Some countries have already made progress on building these institutions (see annex 2).

Proper sequencing will be important. Since some institutions are not necessary until the countries become EU member states, it is important to strategically plan capacity and institution building and give priority to areas on the basis of EU requirements, their usefulness for strengthening public support to agriculture, and the possibility of supporting them with EU pre-accession funding. For example, establishing a Farm Register is needed to develop an IACS and a FADN, which are needed only later as a member state.

Annex 2. Progress in Establishing EU–compliant Institutions

Progress in establishing EU–compliant institutions differs across the Western Balkan countries (table A2.1). fYR Macedonia, an EU candidate country, is most advanced, having begun establishing all of them. All other countries have rightly made the Paying Agency a priority, and some have started preparations for a FADN. The most complex structure, the IACS, requires data on land use, land cadastre system, livestock identification and registration, and the farm register to be integrated. Although the system is needed only for EU accession, countries should still begin preparing.[25] New EU member states often underestimated the time and money needed to develop the system. Their experiences can provide valuable lessons on institution building, time required to prepare for accessing EU IPARD funds, cost of administering the funds, administration cost, and best practices to create demand for funds.

Notes

1. Fan and Rao 2003.
2. In Bosnia and Herzegovina, agricultural spending is fragmented between the entities, cantons and local governments, so comprehensive agricultural spending could be obtained only for one year (2004), and developments over time could not be properly assessed.
3. This funding is for all IPA programs, including transition assistance and institution building, regional and cross-border cooperation, regional development, human resources development, and rural development. Potential candidate countries have access to only two out of these five programs: transition assistance and institution building, and regional and cross-border cooperation. EU candidate countries, such as Croatia, fYR Macedonia, and Turkey, have access to all programs.
4. For more details, see http://ec.europa.eu/agriculture/capreform/infosheets/crocom_en.pdf.
5. For more details, see http://ec.europa.eu/agriculture/healthcheck/index_en.htm.
6. Including modernizing farms, producing safe and high-quality products, ensuring fair and stable incomes for farmers, meeting environmental challenges, fostering supplementary or alternative job-creating activities, and improving living and working conditions and equal opportunities.
7. Up to 25 percent for cereals and other arable crops, up to 40 percent for slaughter premiums, and so on. For more information, see http://ec.europa.eu/agriculture/capreform/infosheets/paymod_en.pdf.

Table A2.1. Countries Are at Different Stages in Developing Institutions Needed for EU Accession and to Modernize Agri-food Support

Country	Integrated Administration and Control System (IACS)	Paying Agency	Farm Accountancy Data Network (FADN)	Rural Development Coordination
Albania	Not yet existing, not mentioned in rural or agriculture strategy.	According to the strategy, an independent paying agency was planned to be established as a forerunner organization in 2007 but has not yet been established.	Not yet existing, not mentioned in either agriculture or rural strategy.	Directorate for Rural Development in Ministry of Agriculture, Food and Consumer Protection. Inter-Ministerial Working Group. National Rural Network.
Bosnia and Herzegovina	Not yet existing, not yet mentioned in strategic documents.	Legislation in preparation according to the Bosnia and Herzegovina Agriculture, Food, and Rural Development Harmonization Strategic Plan (2008–10) but no dates set.	Creation of legislation for unified farm register in preparation. FADN mentioned in the Bosnia and Herzegovina Agriculture, Food, and Rural Development Harmonization Strategic Plan (2008–10), but no dates set.	The Bosnia and Herzegovina Agriculture, Food, and Rural Development Harmonization Strategic Plan (2008–10) mentions the creation of the Rural Development Co-ordination Body and Support Unit under the Ministry of Foreign Trade and Economic Relations for 2008/09.
Macedonia, fYR	Preparations have started. Operational in 2008/09.	Established and in the process of certification, expected by the end of 2008.	To be completed by the end of 2008.	The Ministry of Agriculture, Forestry, and Water Management is the lead coordinating agency for rural development. Inter-Institutional Co-ordination body for Rural Development policy, planning and monitoring planned for 2007/08.
Montenegro	Start implementation in first half of 2008.	Start implementation in first half of 2008.	Start implementation in first half of 2008.	The strategy mentions the need for coordination but does not suggest mechanisms.
Serbia	Not yet started and not mentioned in the strategy.	To be established by the end of 2008.	Not yet started. Establishment of farm registry is in process, to be completed by the end of 2008.	Strategy sees the Ministry of Agriculture, Forestry, and Water Management in charge of coordinating rural development but does not formulate coordination mechanisms. According to the strategy, a Rural Development Agency was planned for 2005 and legally created in 2004 but is not yet operational.

Source: Agriculture and rural strategy documents of Albania, Bosnia and Herzegovina, fYR Macedonia, Montenegro, and Serbia.

8. For more details, see http://ec.europa.eu/agriculture/capreform/infosheets/crocom_en.pdf.

9. This means 33 percent in 2005, 25 percent in 2006, and 20 percent in the years following. Modulation will not apply in new EU member states until direct payments reach EU levels (scheduled for 2013) For more details, see http://ec.europa.eu/agriculture/capreform/infosheets/modul_en.pdf.

10. Fan and Rao 2003; Lopez and Galinato 2007.

11. In Bosnia and Herzegovina direct subsidies for various agricultural products have been provided in both the country's political entities and its cantons since 2004. Production-linked support accounted for more than 70 percent of the Federation of Bosnia and Herzegovina's agricultural support in 2006, compared with almost 90 percent of agricultural support in the Republika Srpska. Although no time series are available for agricultural spending at lower levels of government, anecdotal evidence reveals that cantons and municipalities have also increased spending on subsidies.

12. European Commission 2006a.

13. No country in the Western Balkans has fully developed and implemented a national rural development plan. fYR Macedonia recently developed a plan to prepare for the EU IPARD program, and other countries are following suit. Integrated rural development is Albania's main agricultural policy objective, but concrete measures are still being developed. While there is some evidence that rural development planning is already occurring at the cantonal and municipal levels, rural development planning at the entity level in Bosnia and Herzegovina will be initiated only in 2009. Serbia implemented a rural development program from 2004–07, and a national rural development program was drafted in 2007 for implementation in 2008. In Montenegro rural development measures in 2008 included several programs for individual subsectors. The Ministry of Agriculture, Forestry and Water Management is focusing on consistency with EU priorities and procedures.

14. These include the dairy sector, a program to enhance land use in mountain areas, support to the fishery sector, and support to establish new orchards and vineyards.

15. World Bank 2007d.

16. World Bank 2006a and 2006b.

17. See Fock 2007 and Tillier 2006a, 2006b, 2006c, and 2007 for agriculture public expenditure reviews, and World Bank 2002, 2003c, 2006e, 2006f, and 2006g for public expenditure and institutional reviews.

18. World Bank 2007d.

19. World Bank 2006a.

20. In Bosnia and Herzegovina, public spending and fiscal management are fragmented across several government actors, including the main layers of government in each political entity (entity government, cantons, and municipalities in the Federation of Bosnia and Herzegovina and entity government and municipalities in the Republika Sprska), the state government, and extrabudgetary funds (including health insurance and pension funds) in both entities. In addition, there are a variety of off-budget foreign-donor-funded fiscal activities or aid programs.[0]

21. European Commission 2007d.

22. For more information, see http://www.hm-treasury.gov.uk/spending_review/spend_plancontrol.cfm (Government of the United Kingdom 2008).

23. Private contributions may finance up to 50 percent of the total eligible cost of the investment under the EU IPARD program. Public aid—from the EU budget (up to 75 percent of the public aid) and from the national budget (at least 25 percent of the public aid)—finances at least 50 percent.

24. Estimates presented in World Bank 2006a.

25. Ongoing projects financed by the World Bank in Bosnia and Herzegovina, fYR Macedonia, Montenegro, and Serbia provide targeted investment support for this alignment process with EU institutional requirements: Bosnia and Herzegovina Agriculture and Rural Development Project (2008–12); Macedonia Agriculture Strengthening and Accession Project (2007–11); Montenegro Institutional Development and Agriculture Strengthening Project (2009–13); and Serbia Transition Agriculture Reform Project (2008–11).

CHAPTER 7

Improving Public Services in Agriculture

In undertaking the challenges in this report—improving competitiveness, promoting rural development, adapting to climate change, and improving food safety—farmers and processors need help. However, few of the needed research, education, extension, and information services are generally provided by the private sector. And even when the private sector does provide services, such as with extension services in the Netherlands,[1] the government continues to provide information and awards contracts to the private sector to provide the public services. Accordingly, governments in the Western Balkans still have an important role in providing support services that are key to improving the agri-food sector's competitiveness.

Studies suggest that investment in farm advisory services and applied research can bring high economic rates of return, often boosting output more than other public spending on agriculture can, including subsidies.[2] Returns on research and development investment average 43 percent a year, with high returns in all world regions.[3] Investments in research led to the green revolution which mitigated the food crisis in the 1970s. However, these returns depend on the extent to which investments meet the needs of small farmers and the rural sector. Education can also have high returns. But also here the quality of spending is paramount. This chapter looks at public provision of agricultural support services, information systems, extension, and education and research—and identifies ways to maximize the impact of expenditures on these services.

Key Messages

- Effective extension services can help farmers increase competitiveness and productivity, respond to new circumstances, and better manage their businesses.
- A multifaceted approach—involving the public sector, nongovernmental organizations, rural producer organizations, and private sector service providers—might be the best choice in the medium term for delivering agricultural extension services.
- Agricultural information systems are important for better decision-making by governments, producers, and other market actors.
- Agricultural education and research systems should cater to the new demands of a modern agri-food sector and pursue opportunities for regional and international collaboration and partnerships.

Public Agricultural Support Services

Public agricultural support services include agricultural extension and information systems, such as agricultural statistics, market information, and farm management information.

Agricultural Extension Services

Widening the Scope of Extension Services. Effective extension services help farmers increase competitiveness and productivity, better manage their businesses, and respond to new circumstances such as changing market requirements, food safety concerns, and climate change. In the Western Balkans extension services also have to prepare the agri-food and rural sector for EU accession and the reformed CAP. These challenges require countries to develop demand-oriented and efficient agricultural extension (or, more generally, advisory) services that help farmers and processors compete under EU conditions and facilitate broad-based access to EU IPARD funds. Extension services for market-oriented agricultural development as well as rural development for the noncommercial sector will be needed. Issues such as environmentally sustainable agriculture will be gaining importance, as will business planning, economic and technical training, and assistance in applying for funds and taking advantage of economic opportunities. In the framework of the reformed CAP, direct payments are provided to farmers only if environmental, animal welfare, and food safety regulations are followed (see chapter 6). This "cross-compliance" regulation requires extension systems to support farmers in implementing these regulations.

Existing extension systems in the Western Balkans are not yet in a position to provide all these services. They have traditionally focused on production technologies for crops and livestock, and many now administer support programs. But extension needs to be viewed in a wider rural development context, including agricultural production but also a knowledge and information system for rural people. This is especially so in the Western Balkans, where a small number of commercial farmers will coexist with a much larger number of rural residents carrying out nonfarm activities and providing nonfarm services.

Efforts are under way to reform agricultural extension services or establish new ones throughout the region, and extension systems are slowly being reoriented to provide more demand-based and sustainable services. For example, the National Extension Agency in fYR Macedonia has widened its focus to cover marketing, business planning, and quality standards and to carry out a farm monitoring program.[4] But despite substantial investment in facilities and training, financial constraints limit its capacity, due to a combination of minimal self-financing and insufficient government funding. In Montenegro the extension system provides market information and technical advice to crop and livestock producers and implements the Ministry of Agriculture, Forestry, and Water Management's support programs.[5] In Bosnia and Herzegovina a fully functioning system is not yet in place.[6]

Extension strategies should be defined for the delivery of services, taking into account the farm and rural structure, the type of services to be provided, the role of the public and private sectors, the level of decentralization, and the requirements of EU accession. For example, Hungary established its extension services based on a global review of extension services prepared under the auspices of the FAO.[7] The review enabled the government to address the different needs of small- and large-scale farmers and directed extension support accordingly. Stakeholder involvement is also important, both in developing strategies and in guiding implementation of extension activities. In Estonia a National Agricultural Extension Task Force consisting of farmers, advisors, and public officials was established to develop relevant strategies.[8] Later, an informal extension concept group of major stakeholders carried out this function. Strategies should include a comprehensive monitoring and evaluation program to determine the outreach and impact of services.

Adopting a Multifaceted Approach to Delivering Agricultural Extension Services. There is no universal prescription for delivering and managing extension services. Approaches range from fully public to fully commercialized services. Public extension services can provide a wide range of programs, including farm and natural resources management,[9] but they may be unresponsive to farmer needs, lack ownership among intended beneficiaries, fail to reach poor and female farmers, suffer limitations in the quality of field and technical staff, and have high and unsustainable public costs. Public extension services can also be politicized, and frequent changes in the leadership and prevailing political interests can delay the development of sound extension strategies.[10]

Private extension services are intrinsically more demand-oriented. They may have better access to superior technologies and are better placed to provide farmers information that complements new technologies.[11] But privatizing extension and introducing fees may reduce demand for services and change the client structure, with much higher demand among large farms than among small farms.[12] Many small, semi-subsistence farms lack the financial means to procure private extension services. Options should thus be considered to keep appropriate extension services within their reach.

Various intermediate options involve having different levels of cost recovery and cost-sharing between extension services and clients; devolving control to local government units; contracting service delivery to private firms, nongovernmental organizations, or cooperatives and farmer organizations; and supporting farmers' self-help groups.[13] In the Western Balkans agricultural extension is still largely provided by the public sector, although private advisors, farmer associations, and agri-businesses are working increasingly with farmers. Although a fully private system is not feasible now, approaches based on public funding of services contracted to private local suppliers may be an effective avenue for the Western Balkans to meet the needs of small farmers. Even in the Netherlands, some 60–70 percent of extension is still publicly funded by contracting private suppliers to carry out public good extension activities.

A multifaceted extension approach involving the public sector, nongovernmental organizations, rural producer organizations, and private suppliers may be the best choice in the Western Balkans in the medium term. It can encourage competition among providers and offer a range of local options to clients. In Estonia, for example, extension services and information are provided by private suppliers, the farm unions in each county, the Estonian Farmers' Federation, the associations of agricultural producers, the rural economy specialists of county governments, the national Training and Advisory Center, and the Ministry of Agriculture's Agricultural Registers and Information Board (box 7.1).[14]

All professional agricultural advisors are members of the Estonian Association of Agricultural Advisors. In Hungary, advice and information can be obtained from the village advisors of the local Ministry of Agriculture offices, from advisors in the county offices of the Hungarian Chamber of Agriculture, Agricultural Educational Institutes, demonstration farms, professional advisory centers, agricultural nongovernmental organizations, and private businesses.[15]

Some cost recovery is possible in extension services, but there is currently little in the Western Balkans. The Macedonia National Extension Agency and the Biotechnical Institute in Montenegro do not charge for services, partly because it is widely held that farmers are not in a position to pay. But a small contribution of at least 10 percent may be feasible. In Armenia, for example, the district advisory centers recover 14 percent of costs, on average, and the national center more than 20 percent, through sales of newspapers and publications, consulting activities for private clients, and various contracts.[16] In Hungary, farmers are charged for services based on income. Those with low incomes can participate in group extension activities for free, intermediate-income farmers may receive a subsidy of 35–75 percent for individual advice, and large-scale farmers pay 100 percent.[17]

Other Challenges. More needs to be done to reach the large number of small farmers. The Western Balkan countries have a high ratio of farmers

Box 7.1

Different Contracting Arrangements for Different Farmers in Estonia

The Estonian Ministry of Agriculture launched national agricultural advisory services in 1995 and an advisory subsidy in 1996. The advisory services are provided to farmers on an individual and group basis under different contracting agreements. The cost-sharing varies by type and size of contract: individual services farmers pay 15 percent for smaller contracts, and 50 percent for larger contracts. For group services the participants must cover at least 20 percent of the total cost. Training days, seminars, demonstrations, and publications are also cofinanced by the government. Businesses, universities, and institutes can apply for funds to provide these services.

Source: Loolaid 2002.

to extension specialists. Albania, the most extreme case, has some 245 agricultural specialists to serve some 450,000 small farmers. Clearly, the extension service cannot reach all farmers under these circumstances. To address this issue, some 120 local agricultural information centers have been established, and mass media, such as local newspapers and television, are used to provide information to a wider audience. There is also scope for the government to introduce a system to contract private providers and other sources such as universities and institutes for the delivery of specific information (for example, in food safety issues) rather than always using public extension services.

The quality of extension services needs to improve. Better training and skills are needed for extension staff to collaborate effectively with farmers and apply technical knowledge to site-specific socioeconomic and agronomic conditions rather than delivering prepackaged messages. Extension workers need training in participatory methods of working with clients. Access to timely information and continuous updating of extension staff, both public and private, are also required. Most important, extension workers need farm financial management skills, particularly in investment and gross margin analysis and risk assessment. And the development of an advisory certification system through assessment and examination by an appointed professional institution will be necessary.

New information and communication technologies remain underutilized. Extension systems in the Western Balkans have yet to fully exploit the falling costs and increasing capacity of information systems. Internet-based information services and short-message-service–based market information services can be a cost effective and efficient way to link rural populations to information. In Estonia, rural information centers in almost all communities are linked to a national agricultural information center that provides a range of information electronically.[18] The network has links with organizations such as banks, insurance companies, and commercial companies promoting their services through the Internet.

Agricultural Information Systems Can Improve Public Policies and Markets

Effective information systems are an important tool for informed decision making by governments, producers, and other market actors. They allow governments to evaluate policy and program outcomes, improve budget management, and become more responsive to stakeholders through the provision of key information such as market prices and market developments. This should be distinguished from information that will need to be provided for the EU, such as agricultural market information systems, statistics, and economic accounts. Some promising initiatives have taken place with agricultural market and price information systems in the region, but further improvement is still urgently needed in agricultural statistics and information systems.

New systems required for EU accession can facilitate better systems and databases for domestic policy and business decision making. The main components of the EU agricultural policy information systems are Eurostat's agricultural statistics program (comprising some 30 agricultural statistics domains), the agriculture market information system, the FADN, and the IACS, including the farm registry, for CAP implementation. The basic components are the same for all EU member states, although the institutional setting may differ. Close cooperation with new EU member states could help the Western Balkan countries establish sound information systems using a stepwise approach.

Agricultural Statistics. Accurate data on the number and characteristics of farm households are key to preparing agricultural policies and designing support programs. Private farming was not well covered by official agricultural statistics before 1990, and not all Western Balkan countries have detailed agricultural censuses for recent years. Several other issues complicate sound policy analysis. The definitions of statistical units (farms) and agricultural labor inputs (classification of agricultural employment, annual work unit) are not the same across the region and are not fully harmonized with Eurostat definitions, making comparison difficult. Data on private small-scale farming, agricultural production structures, and rural areas are weak, and systematic problems with agricultural statistics remain (box 7.2). Economic and political upheavals have left structural breaks and interruption of time series, and changes in methodologies complicate analysis and comparison. In addition, statistics on the food processing industry and rural development are not comprehensive and need more emphasis.

The EU's agriculture information system is a set of data and analyses interconnected through harmonized methods and classification of activities and commodities. The system closely follows international classifications, which allows for worldwide comparability and transparency. The institutions responsible for its components are not specified, so EU member states are free to delegate responsibility, with most relying on collaboration between the ministry of agriculture and the statistical office.

The European Commission's Directorate for Agriculture and Rural Development has a separate unit for economic analysis and modeling that issues impact assessments and medium-term outlooks. Each EU

Box 7.2

Agricultural Statistics Are Not Updated Regularly

Livestock and crop production. Long-term trends are available for most countries, but reliability for recent years is problematic. Production levels and volumes are difficult to estimate due to the high share of semisubsistence and subsistence farming.

Agri-food trade. Data are available for all countries, but measurement of intraregional trade in some places is still difficult (Montenegro and Serbia, Kosovo and Albania, Bosnia Herzegovina and Serbia).

Supply balances. Supply balances are not yet regularly made.

Agricultural structures and farm register. A recent farm census was conducted in fYR Macedonia in 2007, but there are no regular structural surveys, and the whole region lacks comprehensive statistical farm registers. Administrative registers are being set up.

Agro-monetary statistics. Economic statistics in agriculture are generally weak.
- *Agricultural price statistics.* Only part of production is marketed and subject to market prices. Problems remain measuring inflation. There are no comprehensive producer price surveys.
- *Economic accounts for agriculture.* No comprehensive implementation of economic accounts for agriculture exists in the region, though fYR Macedonia has made a start.
- *Agricultural labor input statistics.* All data on agricultural labor inputs are based on estimates. Definitions of agricultural employment and farms are unclear.

member state must have sufficient tools and capacities for evaluating policy proposals coming from this unit and for assessing impacts and monitoring developments. Most ministries of agriculture in the Western Balkans have established or are starting to establish similar units. Effective links with universities and relevant research institutes such as Institutes for Agricultural Economics should be developed for this purpose. Cross-border cooperation and coordination, as well as exchange of analysts, can also be extremely valuable.

Agriculture Market Information Systems. Agriculture market information systems are designed for regular collection and processing of agricultural product market and price data to provide relevant information on prices and quantities traded internally and externally. This is very important for farm and agro-business decisionmaking and policy analysis support. Market and price data are also needed for the CAP. All accession countries need to establish an operational system for monitoring agricultural markets, allowing for ontime price and market volume reporting to the European Commission's Directorate for Agriculture and Rural Development.

Agriculture market information systems are generally poorly developed in the Western Balkans. Albania's Agricultural Market Information System, developed with support from Germany's GTZ, collects, processes, and distributes data on the most important agricultural products and regions at the farm-gate and wholesale levels.[19] In Bosnia and Herzegovina a USAID project is attempting to improve farmer information on market developments by preparing subsector profiles, market studies, and reports on key commodities, and by providing market information and analysis.[20] In Serbia the U.S. Department of Agriculture (USDA) is supporting the extension service's development of an agriculture marketing information system network, known as STIPS, which aims to assess and improve price reporting from grains and feed markets from 18 locations.[21] More work is still needed to establish fully coordinated and EU-compliant agriculture market information systems in the region.

Agriculture market information systems should collect, process, publish, and distribute information in cooperation with other institutions such as the statistical office, agricultural extension services, veterinary services, the meat processing industry, wholesale markets, and agricultural producer associations. The system can be organized by a centralized body responsible for all agricultural products, or it can be delegated to different producer associations. Experience in most EU member states has demonstrated that a well-organized, centralized system can meet the needs of the various market stakeholders and administrations. Separate systems tend to be a "closed shop," serving only selected market participants. But when stakeholder interest organizations have enough capacity to be recognized as official producer organizations by the ministry of agriculture, transferring specific market information activities to these organizations can be considered. Experience from the new EU member states has shown that it takes at least four to five years to establish an agriculture market information system and that the system is generally managed by the ministry of agriculture, research institutes, universities, and paying agencies.

Farm Accountancy Data Network (FADN). Farm data systems provide essential information on production, gross margins, land, labor, and capital requirements (including seasonal labor requirements), inputs (fertilizers, manure, pesticides), and net income. They also help extension personnel, farmers, planners, and research workers develop budgets, farm plans, input-output coefficients and production elasticity, and production function estimates. The FADN is an important component of the EU's agricultural information system and a basic tool used in the implementation of the CAP.[22] Data from the network provide an annual determination of incomes on agricultural holdings, a business analysis of agricultural holdings, and an evaluation of the planned modification of the CAP. Derived from national surveys, the network is the only source of harmonized microeconomic data. In most EU member states the network is managed by the ministry of agriculture, a research institute, or an extension service.

Currently, the collection of farm management information is limited in the Western Balkans, and no countries have yet established a FADN. In fYR Macedonia the National Extension Agency established a Farm Monitoring System to collect data from a permanent network of farms. This system could be considered as a forerunner of the FADN, although its budget has limited its scope. Data on income, yields, and expenses are collected on a monthly basis by 100 extension staff from 450 farms selected by size and entrepreneurial activity. The data are entered into the National Extension Agency's database and used to provide immediate advice on farm management and other economic issues to network participants (and increasingly to other farmers as well). Data may also be used for reference by extension officers and for policy analysis. This approach could form a sound basis for establishing FADN systems throughout the region.

Integrated Administration and Control System (IACS). Member states are required to collect data on agricultural holdings as specified in Commission Regulation No. 2237/77. A distinction should be made between a farm register established as a statistical register, which is generally maintained by the statistical office and forms the basis for sampling and implementing agricultural statistics, or as an administrative register, serving the main purpose of managing support payments in agriculture. The basic EU requirements concerning administrative farm registers are in the context of payments administration and control. Direct payments must be paid using the IACS,[23] and a single system to record the identity of each farmer is a compulsory part of the system.[24] Because the system covers the whole agri-food sector (except very small units), it can also serve as an information system for policy analysis and other purposes.

The usual practice within EU member states is for the farm register and the integrated accounting and control system to be managed by the ministry of agriculture, paying agency, or statistical office.

Agricultural Education

In the agri-food sector demand for skills is rising as better technologies are introduced and markets become more discerning. Adequate agricultural education systems that satisfy this demand are thus needed to stimulate growth and competitiveness. Some capacity for such systems already exists in the Western Balkans. For example, Serbia has a comprehensive agricultural education system through several university faculties and agricultural vocational schools. There are faculties of agriculture, veterinary medicine, and forestry at the University of Belgrade and a faculty of agriculture at Novi Sad University. Serbia also has about 60 agricultural middle schools that teach various aspects of agriculture and food technologies through a program designed and implemented by the Ministry of Education. Albania has faculties of agriculture, veterinary medicine, and forestry at the Agricultural University of Tirana, a faculty of agronomy at the University of Korce, and 11 agricultural vocational schools, including a forestry school and a veterinary school. The system is under the authority of the Ministry of Education and Science. There are also agricultural and veterinary faculties in Skopje and a network of agricultural schools in fYR Macedonia, and agricultural faculties in Sarajevo, Banja Luka, and Mostar in Bosnia and Herzegovina.

Despite the substantial network of agricultural schools in the Western Balkans, demand for agricultural technical education is declining for several reasons, including limited employment opportunities in agriculture, low salaries, migration, and limited relevance of the curriculum. In fYR Macedonia 1,190 students were enrolled in 10 schools in 2003/04, but every year more than 30 percent of places remained unfilled.[25] In Albania, enrollment declines each grade, and at least 2 or 3 of the 11 schools are becoming nonviable.[26] Schools still focus on large farms and public sector jobs, rather than the new community of small and medium-size farmers and rural service providers, in terms of curricula, education, and qualification standards. The education system also needs to support rural business development, including processing, storage, packaging, transport, and marketing. In addition, the standalone nature of most agricultural faculties hampers the possibility of interdisciplinary studies, which are important in sectors relevant to EU policies (such as cross-compliance, environmental issues, and rural development). Agricultural faculties are not fully involved in national or international research activities (see also chapter 5), and cooperation between agricultural ministries and research institutions should be improved. University representatives are only rarely involved in elaborating policy strategies and concepts. Closer involvement would also improve the quality of agricultural education at the universities.

More regional and international collaboration and partnerships would strengthen programs. Education establishments in the region, especially the universities, collaborate with many universities in Europe and the United States, some supported by EU programs and other donor activities. This collaboration can bring new ideas and perspectives and should continue to be developed. Regional collaboration can also bring significant opportunities for faculty and student exchange programs, joint degrees, quality assurance, use of external examiners, and other collaborative activities. Regional centers of excellence in specific topics, particularly in graduate education and research, also hold promise. For example, the establishment of veterinary and forestry faculties or fisheries programs at agricultural universities throughout the Western Balkans would not be cost-effective, and should be limited to a few institutions.

The EU's Bologna process is a major opportunity to further improve the quality of agricultural higher education. It aims to align the higher education structure and increase the quality of courses so that qualifications are transferable throughout Europe. The main elements are a three-cycle system (bachelor's degree, master's degree, doctorate), quality assurance, and recognition of qualifications and periods of study. The EU's Tempus and Erasmus programs further support these efforts. Universities across the Western Balkans are currently adjusting their agricultural education systems to EU standards as part of this process.[27] But the reorganization and refocusing of curricula, teaching practices, quality, and still have some way to go. Specifically, teaching in agricultural economics and business, marketing, agricultural policy, environmental and natural resource management, and biotechnology needs continued upgrading.

Agricultural Research

Agricultural research is becoming increasingly vital in helping farmers boost productivity, especially given the global food crisis; improve product quality and safety; and adapt to climate change. But the level and quality of expenditures are generally insufficient in the Western Balkan countries. Agricultural research and development spending across the region is usually less than 1 percent of agricultural GDP, compared with 1.41 percent in 1981 and 2.36 percent in 2000 in developed countries.[28]

Reforms are happening, but further changes are need to improve efficiency and impact. The region's research systems were originally designed to provide technical packages to large farms. Priorities have shifted slightly, but most research has limited relevance to the new class of smaller private farmers and tends to focus on on-station rather than on-farm trials, partly because of limited funds. Many research stations and institutes lack adequate facilities, equipment, and budgets and have aging staff. Cooperation and links between research and educational institutions, agricultural policy formulation institutions, extension services and clients remain weak. Communication and knowledge transfer are often informal, so potentially useful research results are not always readily available to producers.

Agricultural research spending needs to focus on clearly identified priorities and farmer needs. High-value crops, including early vegetables and soft fruits, such as raspberries, have potential in some areas of the Western Balkans to supply the tourist market, the growing domestic market, and early-season markets in more northerly regions. With these crops, small farmers could derive significant income from smaller plots. While high-value crops are likely to become increasingly important to the rural economy, selection and testing of mainstream crops (including cereals) must continue, particularly in order to maintain disease and pest resistance and provide basic and pre-basic seed of locally adapted varieties for seed producers. As already highlighted in chapter 5, countries of the Western Balkans should also start aligning their national agricultural research programs with the structure and priorities areas set out in EU Research Framework Programs and seize upon the opportunities to actively participate in current and future collaborative research projects

Limited funds may be better used for applied research rather than more basic research (box 7.3). Applied research includes a greater focus on on-farm and onsite trials with farmer involvement, and can be widened to include storage, packaging, and marketing technologies.

Private research is unlikely to play a major role in the immediate future, but it will become more important in the long term. No figures are available for the Western Balkans alone, but 94 percent of the agricultural research and development in developing countries is conducted by the public sector.[29] The proper structures must be in place to encourage private investment in research. For example, for seed companies to

Box 7.3

Albania's Steps to Reform the Agricultural Research System

Albania's agricultural research system reforms have attempted to address the concerns of limited funding. After a long consultation, the research network has shrunk from 18 research institutes early in the transition to 5 regional agricultural technology transfer centers today. Basic research responsibilities have been transferred to the universities, particularly the Agricultural University of Tirana, and several institutes were closed or merged. Some facilities remain as service centers—for example, the food safety laboratories. The regional centers focus on applied research aligned with the needs of farmers and improved links with the extension system. Advisory boards include representatives of local farmers and rural businesses helping to define priorities and programs. The Ministry of Agriculture's Department of Extension, Science and Information is now to oversee the system as a whole and to monitor expenditures and outcomes. Significant investment in facilities has taken place using government and donor funds. The streamlining has resulted in increasing funds available for research operations. These moves are in the right direction, but reforms are still at an early stage, and it remains to be seen whether the actual implementation in the field, and the efficiency and impact of the reorganized research system, can be maintained over the long term.

introduce and release varieties, an important private activity, an effective regulatory structure to protect intellectual property rights and provide investment returns is needed. Legislation is in place to protect seed varieties in the Western Balkans, and there are several seed testing laboratories certified by the International Seed Testing Association (ISTA), but stronger regulatory enforcement is often needed. Lower barriers for product testing and registration regimes will also facilitate private investment.

Many research stations and institutes are developing valuable links with both international research organizations, including the Consultative Group on International Agriculture Research (CGIAR) institutions and regional partners. This should continue, with added emphasis on linking domestic research and educational institutions, extension services, and farmer clients. Public research institutions carry out some extension activities, but these are limited mainly to publicly funded training and educational activities linked to their research and occasionally to providing advice on an individual basis.

Duplication of research activities throughout the Western Balkans is unlikely to be cost-effective. Regional centers of excellence that share research results, information, and resources may be useful. One example is the Maize Research Institute in Zemun Polje, Serbia, which develops maize hybrids and varieties of high-yielding potential and quality for different growing conditions and various needs and purposes.[30] The institute manages the European maize database and has a gene bank with some 12,000 accessions from 15 European contributors. This institute is the lead organization for maize research in the region and could be the focus for all public maize development activities. Similar centers of excellence should be developed.

Notes

1. Proost and Duijsings 2002.
2. Lopez and Galinato 2007.
3. Alston and others 2000.
4. The agency, in Bitola, is independent of the Ministry of Agriculture. It has six regional centers and 30 branches across the country. It employs 130 staff, 100 of whom are technical advisors.
5. Extension activities are provided through the Biotechnical Institute by two sister services, the Plant Production Extension Service and the Livestock Selection Service. The services are entirely financed from the Ministry of Agriculture budget. Each service has around 20 staff, mostly in six regional offices.
6. Extension offices were established throughout Bosnia and Herzegovina in 2000 with EU support. Responsibilities included designing business plans and providing other advisory services for farmers. In the Republika Srpska the system is still in place and includes municipal-based advisors in most areas, supported by a central support unit in Banja Luka. Though appreciated, the service is poorly equipped, underfunded and understaffed. In the Federation of Bosnia and Herzegovina the system was established at the canton level, with no central service. But it is largely nonoperational due to limited interest from cantons.
7. Adams 2001.
8. World Bank 2004.
9. Swanson and Sami 2002.
10. World Bank 1996.
11. Swanson and Sami 2002.
12. In the last year of free public extension in Thuringia, Germany, some 80 percent of farmers sought advice. When private extension was introduced in January 1998, this figure fell to about 13 percent, with half the clients being large farms of more than 500 hectares. About 88 percent of large farming enterprises paid for advice compared with only 9.3 percent of small farms of less than 500 hectares (Currle and others 2002).

13. World Bank 1996.

14. Ministry of Agriculture of Estonia 2002.

15. Cser and others 2007.

16. World Bank 2008h.

17. In 2004 low-income farmers were those earning less than 3 million forints a year, and intermediate farmers those earning 3–50 million forints (Ministry of Agriculture and Rural Development of Hungary 2004).

18. World Bank 1996.

19. The Albanian Agriculture Market Information System provides numerous market reports, publications, and data tables; see http://www.albamis.com/index_en.html.

20. See the USAID's Linking Agricultural Markets to Processors Website at http://www.usaidlamp.ba/en/index.html.

21. See the Agricultural Market Information System of Serbia Website at www.stips.minpolj.sr.gov.yu/.

22. The concept of the FADN was launched in 1965, when Council Regulation 79/65 established the legal basis for the organization of the network. The scope and format of the network's data are detailed in the Commission Regulation No 3272/82 of 6 December 1982 amending Regulation No 2237/77 on the form of farm return to be used for determining incomes of agricultural holdings. Holdings are selected to take part in the survey based on sampling plans established at the level of each region in the European Union. The survey does not cover all EU agricultural holdings—only those considered commercial based on their size.

23. EU Regulation 1781/03 (Article 17), and EU Regulation 1698/05.

24. EU Regulation 1782/03 (Article 18) and EU Regulation 796/04 (Article 5).

25. FAO 2007b.

26. Bajraba 2005.

27. For example, the Agricultural University of Tirana is undergoing a restructuring according to the Bologna Declaration. Since 2005/06 the university has been shifting its program toward the 3+2+3 schedule (bachelor's degree, master's degree, and doctorate) and toward diploma recognition and equalization. The university is boosting cooperation by carrying out joint scientific research projects, by exchanging academic and administrative staff and students, and by organizing joint seminars, workshops, and conferences.

28. World Bank 2006d.

29. Pardey and others 2007.

30. For more information, see the Maize Research Institute Zeman Polje Website at http://www.mrizp.co.yu/index-en.php.

References

Adams, G. 2001. "Effective Management in Extension Advisory Services in Central and Eastern European Countries." Paper presented at the Conference on the Central and Eastern European Agricultural Extension, May 14–18, 2000, Eger, Hungary. http://www.fao.org/sd/2001/KN0303a2_en.htm

Agra Europe. 2006. "Regional Trade Pact for SE Europe." *Agra Europe Weekly* 2238. EP10 (December 15). http://www.agra-net.com/portal/puboptions .jsp?Option=menu&pubId=ag002

Albanian Agriculture Market Information System. Official website. http://www .albamis.com/index_en.html#

Alston, J. M., C. Chan-Kang, M. C. Marra, P. E. Pardey, and T. J. Wyatt. 2000. *A Meta-analysis of Rates of Return to Agricultural R&D*. Research Report 113. Washington, DC: International Food Policy Research Institute. http://www .ifpri.org/pubs/abstract/113/rr113.pdf

Bajraba, K. 2005. "The Agriculture Higher Schools towards Transforming into Extension Services and Training Centers." Study for the Albania Agriculture Services Project. The World Bank. Washington, DC.

Baourakis, G., C. Lakatos, and A. Xepapadeas. 2006. "From Dayton to Brussels: A Presentation of the Balkan's Status Quo." TRADEAG Working Paper 06/08. Mediterranean Agronomic Institute of Chania. Chania, Greece.

Baylis, M., and A. Githeko. 2006. *The Effects of Climate Change on Infectious Diseases of Animals.* State of Science Review for Foresight Project Detection and Identification of Infectious Diseases. U.K. Department of Trade and Industry. London, UK.

Binswanger-Mkhize, H. 2008. *Challenges and Opportunities for African Agriculture and Food Security: High Food Prices, Climate Change, Population Growth, and*

HIV and AIDS. Report presented at FAO High-Level Conference on How to Feed the World in 2050, December 15-17, 2008, Rome, Italy. www.fao .org/world/Regional/RNE/morelinks/climate/Africa_Challenges_ ExecutiveSummary_Binswanger1.doc.

Bielza, M., J. Stroblmair, and J. Gallego. 2007. "Agricultural Risk Management in Europe." Paper presented at the 101st EAAE Management of Climate Risks in Agriculture Seminar, July 5–6, 2007, Berlin, Germany http://www .agroinsurance.com/files//bielza.pdf.

Brown, P. K., and M. A. Hepworth. 2002. "A Study of European Land Tax Systems - Second Year Report." Lincoln Institute of Land Policy Working Paper. Lincoln Institute of Land Policy. Cambridge, Massachusetts.

CEEC AGRI Policy. 2006a. "Monitoring of Agricultural Policy, Market and Trade Developments in Bosnia and Herzegovina." D12-1 First 6-monthly report for project 513705. http://www.euroqualityfiles.net/cecap/Report%201/ Section%201%20country%20report/CEECAP%20report%201%20section% 201%20BOSNIA%20HERZEGOVINA.pdf.

———. 2006b. "Structure and Competitiveness of the Milk and Dairy Supply Chain in Hungary." D12-3 Third 6-monthly report for project 513705. http:// www.euroqualityfiles.net/cecap/Report%203/Section%201%20country%20 report/CEECAP%20report%203%20section%201%20HUNGARY.pdf

Central European Land Knowledge Center. 2005. *CELK Newsletter* 7 (July/ August). http://www.4cli.org/celk/wwwcelknew/celk_newsletter/celk%20 hirlevel-newsletter_7.pdf.

Clemens, R. 2004. "Keeping Farmers on the Land: Agri-Tourism in the European Union." Iowa Ag Review Online Volume 10/No 3. http://www.card.iastate .edu/iowa_ag_review/summer_04/article4.aspx.

Cline, W. R. 2007. *Global Warming and Agriculture: Impact Estimates by Country.* Washington, DC: Center for Global Development and Peterson Institute for International Economics.

Critchley, W., and K. Siegert. 1991. *A Manual for the Design and Construction of Water Harvesting Schemes for Plant Production.* AGL/MISC/17/91. Food and Agriculture Organization. Rome, Italy http://www.fao.org/docrep/u3160e/ u3160e00.HTM

Cser, J., J. Kaldi, and J. Kozari. 2007. "Establishment of Regional Advisory Network to Support Farms in the Decision-making Procedure." Academia Scientriarum Lithuaniae. Vilnius, Lithuania.

Currle, J., V. Hoffmann, and A. Kidd. 2002. "Contracting for Agricultural Extension in Thuringia.". In W. M. Rivera and W. Zijp, eds., *Contracting for Agriculture Extension: International Case Studies and Emerging Practices.* Wallingford, UK: CABI Publishing.

Daugaliene, V. 2004. "Preparation for Land Consolidation in Lithuania." Paper presented at the Symposium on Modern Land Consolidation, September 10–11, 2004, Volvic (Clermont-Ferrand), France.

De Janvry, A., and E. Sadoulet. 2007. "Toward a Territorial Approach to Rural Development" *Electronic Journal of Agricultural and Development Economics* 4 (1): 66–98.

Dimitrova, A., ed. 2004. *Driven to Change: The European Union's Enlargement Viewed from the East*. Manchester, UK: Manchester University Press.

Dries, L., and J. F. M Swinnen. 2004. "Foreign Direct Investment, Vertical Integration, and Local Suppliers: Evidence from the Polish Dairy Sector." *World Development* 32 (9): 1525–44.

Dries, L., and N. Noev. 2006. "A Comparative Study of Vertical Coordination in the Dairy Chains in Bulgaria, Poland and Slovakia." Study prepared for The Dynamics of Vertical Coordination in the Agrifood Chains of the Transition Countries of Eastern Europe and Central Asia Project. The World Bank. Washington, DC.

Dries, L., T. Reardon, and J.F.M. Swinnen. 2004. "The Rapid Rise of Supermarkets in Central and Eastern Europe: Implications for the Agrifood Sector and Rural Development." *Development Policy Review* 22 (5): 525–56.

European Commission. 2000. "Enlargement Strategy Paper - Report on Progress towards Accession by Each of the Candidate Countries." COM (2000) 700F. Brussels.

———. 2003. "European Union Financial Report 2002." Office for Official Publications of the European Communities. Luxembourg.

———. 2005. *Report on Budgetary and Financial Management accompanying the Community accounts - Financial Year 2005*. Office for Official Publications of the European Communities. Luxembourg.

———. 2006a. *Risk Issues*. Special Eurobarometer Report 238. Brussels.

———. 2006b. "Study on the State of Agriculture in Five Applicant Countries." Serbia Country Report. Brussels. http://ec.europa.eu/agriculture/analysis/external/applicant/serbia_en.pdf.

———. 2006c. "Study on the State of Agriculture in Five Applicant Countries." Bosnia and Herzegovina Country Report. Brussels. http://ec.europa.eu/agriculture/analysis/external/applicant/bosnia_herzegovina_en.pdf.

———. 2006d. Eurobarometer Survey Report 65. Brussels.

———. 2007a. *Europeans, Agriculture, and the Common Agricultural Policy*. Special Eurobarometer Report 276. Brussels.

———. 2007b. *Green Paper: Adapting to Climate Change in Europe—Options for EU Action*. COM 354 final. Brussels.

————. 2007c. *Instrument for Pre-Accession Assistance (IPA): Multi-Annual Indicative Financial Framework for 2009-2011.* COM(2007) 689 final. Brussels.

————. 2007d. *Support to Sector Programs: Sector Budget Support, Pool Funding, and EC Project Procedures - Guidelines No2.* Tools and Methods Series. Brussels.

————. 2008. *Seventh Research Framework Programme.* Brussels. http://cordis.europa.eu/fp7/kbbe/home_en.html.

European Parliament , European Council, and European Commission. 2006. "Inter-Institutional Agreement between the European Parliament, the Council and the Commission on Budgetary Discipline and Sound Financial Management." Office for Official Publications of the European Communities, Luxembourg.

Eurostat. 2005. "External Trade of Western Balkan Countries." Statistics in Focus 1/2005. Brussels

————. 2008. *Eurostat Statistical Yearbook 2008.* Office for Official Publications of the European Communities, Luxembourg.

Fan, S., and N. Rao. 2003. "Public Spending in Developing Countries: Trends, Determination and Impact." EPTD Discussion Paper 99. International Food Policy Research Institute, Washington, DC.

FAO (Food and Agriculture Organization of the United Nations).

————. 2001. *Former Republic of Yugoslavia: Review of the Sunflower Oil Sector.* FAO Investment Centre and EBRD Cooperation Programme Report 01/050. Rome.

————. 2004. *Review of the Sugar Sector in Serbia and Montenegro.* FAO Investment Centre and EBRD Cooperation Programme Report 6. Rome.

————. 2007a. *Review of the Macedonian Wine Sector.* FAO Investment Centre and EBRD Cooperation Programme Report. Rome.

————. 2007b. Macedonian Agricultural Research and Extension System. Country Report. Paper presented in FAO stakeholder consultation on "Building partnerships for Technology Generation, Assessment and Sharing in Agriculture among West Balkan Countries," June 2007, Rome, Italy. http://www.fao.org/nr/res/wshops/res_ws1_reports_en.htm.

————. 2007c. Review of the Dairy Sector in Montenegro. FAO Investment Centre and EBRD Cooperation Programme Report. Rome.

————. 2008. *Support for Preparation of Proposal on State Land Management in Rural Areas of FYR Macedonia.* Report presented at FIG/FAO/CNG International Seminar on State and Public Sector Land Management, 9–10 September, 2008, Verona, Italy http://www.fig.net/commission7/verona_fao_2008/ppt/10_sept/6_3_georgievski.pdf.

FAO (Food and Agriculture Organization of the United Nations) and UNES-CO IIEP (United Nations Educational, Scientific, and Cultural Organization International Institute for Educational Planning). 2003. *Education for Rural People: Targeting the Poor.* Report of the Aid Agencies Workshop organized on December 12–13, 2002, Rome, Italy.

FAOSTAT. 2008. *Food and Agriculture Organization of the United Nations Statistical Databases and Datasets.* Official website: http://faostat.fao.org/

Fock, K. 2007. "Montenegro Agriculture Expenditure Review." The World Bank, Washington, DC.

Garside, B., J. MacGregor, and B. Vorley. 2008. "Miles Better? How 'Fair Miles' Stack Up in the Sustainable Supermarkets." *Fresh Perspectives* 9 (April). http://www.agrifoodstandards.net/en/filemanager/active?fid=107.

Gerber, L., and R. Giovarelli. 2005. *Land Reform and Land Markets in Eastern Europe.* Food and Agriculture Organization. Rome. http://www.fao.org/docrep/008/y7218t/y7218t0c.htm.

Government of the Republic of Montenegro. 1992. "1992 Law on Agricultural Land." *Official Gazette of the Republic of Montenegro* 15(92) and 50(92).

Government of Serbia. 2008a. *Decree related to Danube Food Group.* Competition Protection Commission. Belgrade, Serbia http://www.kzk.org.yu/download/Resenje%20-%20Danube%20Foods%20Group.pdf.

———. 2008b. *Agricultural Market Information System of Serbia.* Official website: http://www.stips.minpolj.sr.gov.yu/.

Government of the United Kingdom. 2008. "Public Expenditure Planning and Control in the UK—A Brief Introduction." HM Treasury. London. http://www.hm-treasury.gov.uk/spending_review/spend_plancontrol.cfm.

IPCC (Intergovernmental Panel on Climate Change). 2001. *Special Report on Emission Scenarios (SRES).* Prepared by the IPCC for the Third Assessment Report (TAR). Cambridge, UK: Cambridge University Press.

———. 2007a. *Climate Change 2007: Impacts, Adaptation, and Vulnerability.* Contribution of Working Group II to the Fourth Assessment Report of the Intergovernmental Panel on Climate Change. Cambridge, UK: Cambridge University Press.

———. 2007b. *Climate Change 2007: Synthesis Report. Contribution of Working Groups I, II and III to the Fourth Assessment Report of the Intergovernmental Panel on Climate Change.* Geneva, Switzerland.

Kellems, R.O. 2000. *Optimizing Dairy Feed Programmes.* AGRIPPA Journal (December 2000). http://www.fao.org/DOCREP/ARTICLE/AGRIPPA/X9500E02.HTM.

Loolaid, U. 2002. "Estonia: the Role of Contracting for Private Agricultural Advisory services." In *Contracting for Agriculture Extension: International Case*

Studies and Emerging Practices, eds. W. M. Rivera and W. Zijp. Wallingford, UK: CABI Publishing.

Lopez, R., and G. I. Galinato. 2007. "Should Governments Stop Subsidies to Private Goods? Evidence from Rural Latin America." *Journal of Public Economics* 91: 1071–94.

Lukas, Z. 2005. "The Agricultural Land in the New EU Countries: Are There Any Consequences to the Acceptance of the CAP?" *Agricultural Economics—Czech* 51 (5): 225–29.

Maize Research Institute Zeman Polje. 2008. Official website. http://www.mrizp .co.yu/index-en.php.

Marosan, S., and O. Vasovic. 2005. "The State of Cadastre, Land Market, and Real Property Development in Serbia and Montenegro." Presentation delivered at FAO Workshop on the Development of Land Markets and Related Institutions in Central and Eastern European Countries, May 6–7, 2005, Nova Scotia.   http://www.fao.org/regional/seur/events/landmark/docs/marosan_pres .pdf

Marosan, S., M. Trajkovic, V. Djokic, M. Soskic, and Z. Knezevic. 2007. "Land Consolidation and Rural Development in Serbia." Paper presented at FAO Regional Workshop on Land Consolidation, June 25–27, 2007, Prague, Czech Republic.

Ministry of Agriculture of Estonia. 2002. *Estonian Agriculture, Rural Economy and Food Industry.* Tallinn. http://www.agri.ee/public/juurkataloog/ENG/Estonia n%20Agriculture,%20Rural%20Economy%20And%20Food%20Industry.pdf

Ministry of Agriculture and Rural Development of Hungary. 2004. "Hungarian Agriculture and Food Industry in Figures." Paper presented at the 99th Seminar of the European Association of Agriculture Economists, August 24–27, 2004, Bonn, Germany.

Ministry of Health of Albania. 2006. "Analysis of the State of Food and Nutrition in Albania." Directorate of Primary Health Care. Tirana.

Muenz, R. 2007. "Aging and Demographic Change in European Societies: Main Trends and Alternative Policy Options." SP Discussion paper 0703. Social Protection, The World Bank, Washington, DC. http://www.monitoringris .org/documents/tools_reg/agingdemochange.pdf

OECD (Organization for Economic Co-operation and Development). 2007. "SME Policy Index 2007 – Report on the Implementation of the European Charter for Small Enterprises in the Western Balkans." Investment Compact for South East Europe, and European Commission Directorate for Enterprise and Industry. Paris/Brussels. http://www.oecd.org/dataoecd/31/41/38310075 .pdf

Pardey, P.G., J. Alston, J. James, P. Glewwe, E. Binebaum, T. Hurley, and S. Wood. 2007. "Science, Technology and Skills." Background paper for *World Develop-*

ment Report 2008: Agriculture for Development. The World Bank, Washington, DC.

Planet Retail. 2006. "Retail Markets Begin to Consolidate in Ex-Yugoslavia." *Planet Retail Weekly Bulletin* 185.

———. 2007. Planet Retail Database and Datasets. Official website http://www .planetretail.net/Default.aspx

Popp, J., and M. Stauder. 2003. "Land Markets in Hungary." *Agriculture Economics – Czech* 49(4): 173–78.

Proost, J., and P. Duijsings. 2002. "The Netherlands: Going Dutch in Extension, 10 Years of Experiences with Privatized Extension." In W. M. Rivera and W. Zijp, eds., *Contracting for Agriculture Extension: International Case Studies and Emerging Practices.* Wallingford, UK: CABI Publishing.

Psacharopoulos, G., and H. A. Patrinos. 2002. "Returns to Investment in Education: A Further Update." Policy Research Working Paper 2881. The World Bank, Washington, DC.

Quiroga, S., and A. Iglesias. 2007. "Projections of Economic Impacts of Climate Change in Europe." *Economia Agrariay Recursos Naturales* 7 (14): 65–82. http://www.congresoaeea.org/downloads/04Quiroga.pdf

Rabinowicz, E., S. Bajramovic, S. Davidora, and M. Pettersson. 2006. *Competitiveness in the Agricultural Sector of Bosnia and Herzegovina.* SLI Report: 5. Swedish Institute for Food and Agricultural Economics. Lund, Sweden.

Ramasamy, S. 2008. "Agroclimatic Situation in the Balkans." Food and Agriculture Organization, Rome.

Rau, M.-L., and F. van Tongeren. 2006. "Modelling Differentiated Quality Standards in the Agri-food Sector: The Case of Meat Trade in the EU." Paper presented at the 26th International Association of Agricultural Economists Conference, August 12–18, 2006, Brisbane, Australia.

Rawlings, L., and G. Rubio. 2005. "Evaluating the Impact of Conditional Cash Transfer Programs: Lessons from Latin America." *World Bank Research Observer* 20 (1): 29–55. http://wbro.oxfordjournals.org/cgi/content/ abstract/20/1/29.

Reardon, T., G. Vrabec, D. Karakas, and C. Fritsch. 2003. "The Rapid Rise of Supermarkets in Croatia: Implications for Farm Sector Development and Agribusiness Competitiveness Programmes." Michigan State University, East Lansing/Development Alternatives Inc., Washington, DC.

Sallaku, F., and A. Shehu. 2005. "Land Fragmentation and Consolidation in Albania." Agriculture University of Tirana.

SEE News. 2008. "Bulgarian REIT Agro Finance to Issue up to 2.6 Mln € Bond." 10 March 2008.

Snyder, R.L., J. P. Paulo de Melo-Abreu, and S. Matulich. 2005. *Frost Protection: Fundamentals, Practice, and Economics* 2 (10).

Steinfeld, H. and J. Mäki-Hokkonen. 1995. *A Classification of Livestock Production Systems.* Food and Agriculture Organization. Rome, Italy http://www.fao.org/DOCREP/V8180T/v8180T0y.htm

Swanson B.E., and M.M. Samy. 2002. Developing an Extension Partnership among Public, Private and Nongovernmental Organizations. *Journal of International Agricultural and Extension Education* 9(1): 5–10.

The Financial Times. 2008. "Commodity Boom Drives Up Land Values." 24 April 2008.

Tillier, S. 2006a. "Macedonia—Agriculture Public Expenditure Review." The World Bank, Washington, DC.

———. 2006b. "Serbia—Agriculture Public Expenditure Review." The World Bank, Washington, DC.

———. 2006c. "Albania—Agriculture Public Expenditure Review." The World Bank, Washington, DC.

———. 2007. "Bosnia and Herzegovina—Public Spending in Agriculture." The World Bank, Washington, DC.

UNECE (United Nations Economic Commission for Europe). 2002. "Environmental Performance Review: Albania." Environmental Performance Reviews Series 16. Committee on Environmental Policy, Geneva, Switzerland. http://www.unece.org/env/epr/epr_studies/albania.pdf

USDA (United States Department of Agriculture). 1993. World Agriculture Trends and Indicators (1970-1991). Statistical Bulletin No. 861. Economic Research Service. Washington, DC.

UNDP (United Nations Development Programme). 2005. "Formulation of Sector Policy Strategy - Final Report." Strengthening the Marketing of Small Ruminants Project, UNDP Albania.

USAID (United States Agency for International Development). n.d. Linking Agricultural Markets to Producers (LAMP). Official website. http://www.usaidlamp.ba/en/index.html

Washington Post. 2008a. "Mexican Tomato Growers Say Warning Unfair." 11 June 2008.

———. 2008b. "Engineering a Safer Burger." 12 June 2008.

World Bank. 1996. *The World Bank Participation Sourcebook.* Washington, DC.

———. 2002. *Macedonia—Public Expenditure and Institutional Review.* Economic Report 23349. Washington DC.

———. 2003a. "Kosovo Investment Climate Assessment." Washington, DC.

———. 2003b. *Final Report, Republic of Serbia, Agriculture Sector Review*. Washington, DC.

———. 2003c. *Serbia and Montenegro—Public Expenditure and Institutional Review*. Volumes I, II, and III. Washington, DC.

———. 2004. "Estonia: Transition to Private Extension Advisory Services." In *Agriculture Investment Sourcebook*. Washington, DC.

———. 2005. *Drought Management and Mitigation Assessment for Central Asia and the Caucasus*. Report 31990. Washington, DC.

———. 2006a. *Agriculture and EU Accession: Achieving FYR Macedonia's Agricultural Potential*. Report AAA11-MK. Skopje, fYR Macedonia.

———. 2006b. *Supporting Serbia's Agriculture Strategy*. Report 37825-YF. Washington, DC.

———. 2006c. "Benchmarking FDI Opportunities. Investment Horizons: Western Balkans." Washington, DC.

———. 2006d. *World Development Report 2007: Development and the Next Generation*. Report 35999. Washington, DC.

———. 2006e. *Albania Restructuring Public Expenditure to Sustain Growth. A Public Expenditure and Institutional Review*. Volumes I and II. Washington, DC.

———. 2006f. *Bosnia and Herzegovina—Addressing Fiscal Challenges and Enhancing Growth Prospects: A Public Expenditure and Institutional Review*. Report 36156-BA. Washington, DC.

———. 2006g. *Kosovo—Public Expenditure and Institutional Review*. Volumes I and II. Washington, DC.

———. 2007a. "Synthesis Report on South Eastern Europe Countries Disaster Risk." Washington, DC.

———. 2007b. "Escaping the Middle Income Trap: Trade, Integration, and Growth in the Western Balkans." Washington, DC.

———. 2007c. "The Evolution and Impact of EU Regional and Rural Policy." WDR Briefing Note. Washington, DC.

———. 2007d. *Albania. Strategic Policies for a More Competitive Agriculture Sector*. Report AAA18-AL. Washington, DC.

———. 2007e. *World Development Report 2008: Agriculture for Development*. Report 39613. Washington, DC.

———. 2007f. *Connecting to Compete: Trade Logistics in the Global Economy*. Washington, DC.

———. 2008a. *Regional Tertiary Education and Research for South Eastern Europe and Balkans*. Washington, DC.

———. 2008b. *Weather Climate Services in Europe and Central Asia: a Regional Review*. Washington, DC.

———. 2008c. *Doing Business in South East Europe in 2008.* Washington, DC.

———. 2008d. *Shrinking Distance: Identifying Priorities and Assessing Equity Efficiency Trade-Offs with Territorial Development Policies.* Washington, DC.

———. 2008e. *Managing Uncertainty: Adapting to Climate Change in ECA Countries.* Washington, DC.

———. 2008f. *Unleashing Prosperity: Productivity Growth in Eastern Europe and the Former Soviet Union.* Washington, DC.

———. 2008g. *Paying Taxes 2009 – The Global Picture.* Washington, DC.

———. 2008h. "May 2008 Mission Aide-Memoire - Rural Enterprise and Small-scale Agricultural Development Project in Armenia." Washington, DC.

———. 2008i. *Weather and Climate Services in Europe and Central Asia: A Regional Review.* Washington, DC.

———. Forthcoming. *Climate Change, Agriculture and Food Security: Adaptation and Mitigation Hot Spots and Opportunities Informed by Latest Generation Climate Change Model Scenarios.* Washington, DC.

World Economic Forum. 2008. *Global Competitiveness Report 2007–2008.* Geneva, Switzerland.

World Resources Institute. 2003. *Earth Trends Country Profile.* Washington, DC. Official website. http://earthtrends.wri.org/country_profiles/index.php?theme=8

Index

www.ingramcontent.com/pod-product-compliance
Lightning Source LLC
Chambersburg PA
CBHW070243290326
41929CB00046B/2417